From Albion to Shangri-La

DEDICATION

In disorder and without immediate context, this opens the dedication of the collection – to the woman I love, and my best girl. It helps to avoid complication that they are the same person entirely. It adds to the complication altogether that she is the one person that is concerned most with the contents of the book. Concerned that is with the 5 years of assorted declarations of love, lust fuck tidings and here and there the flutterings of a heart and the sleeve it is worn on.

Indiscretion... as with the Books of Albion, there has been a painful and protracted punch up the emotional bracket for my missus...

It is hardly private all this -

And yet she is a private person.

It is drug and oblivious connected or therein conceived - and yet she does not take drugs or imbibe to doolally levels.

There is a steady roll-call of wood nymphs and yet... I love only her. I want only her.

Happy Birthday, dear BouBou. I love you. This is the dedication. Hmmm? I love you.

Peter
The kitchen table
Hamburg   6th June 2014

Preface

by Peter Doherty

Nina,

as requested, I have carefully carved an introduction into the plasticoated thinwood of my extended arm: that I meet, meet and greet the scum fringes and elite of the libraries, lost highways and the streets

aye, the same old faces, all with the two eyes, mostly with two eyes, two faces

fewer graces and skewered taste in the written word, the intellectual dirty hit: they don't write and they don't riot

even then we might make our darker sides light

and invite talent in tonight

even as I type in time to the stereo's crackle and chime, it's a grind, ivory headstones lined in lime -

stereotypical style of English melody sublime

and the crossover between our legends of radio friendless rhyme and the mass of magnificent minds that tend to end up committed to crime

elegantly botched ideas of literary lineages popposturesPrettyhiplickre-RamoneRonetteRootytooty

one by one day by day they will turn away from the end

Nina writes, seen her riot

From Albion to Shangri-La

Journals 2008-2013

Peter Doherty

Transcribed, selected and edited by Nina Antonia

Tenth Anniversary Edition 2024

First published by Thin Man Press London 2014

© Peter Doherty

Peter Doherty is hereby identified as author of these works in accordance with the Copyright, Designs and Patents Acts, 1988. The author has asserted his moral rights. No part of this publication may be reproduced, stored in a retrieval system, or transmitted, in any form or by any means without the prior written permission of the publisher.

A CIP catalogue record for this title is available from the British Library

ISBN 978-1-9997940-2-6

Thin Man Press London

www.thinmanpress.com

All illustrations © Peter Doherty

Cover design/artwork Colin Gibson, Guanografix

Contents

Introduction by Nina Antonia...9

List of Characters...19

From Albion to Shangri-La (Journals)...............................23

Tour Diaries..217

Interview with Peter Doherty by Nina Antonia............239

Introduction

Where does the pied-piper go? The beautiful melodies fade along with the visions of Albion, into history, memory, like the Gods of the old world. For nearly two decades, Peter Doherty has enchanted audiences with a dream first conjured in a childhood of army bases, barracks and barbed wire. The gifted progeny of a well-meant if regimented upbringing, Peter was the only child in class who had to polish his shoes every day. Most of what followed was reaction – a flight from order; proof that he was never meant to be contained. The reoccurring themes of mystical idylls that pepper his work and visions - Albion, Arcadia and Shangri-La – have always promised a retreat from restriction. But as the years rush by, like an excited crowd, even their creator seems less certain of finding sanctuary. 'On the horizon, there's a little piece of land I spy/ Will we go someplace where they know my face?/ Gather round and bear witness to my fall from grace,' he sings on *Fall from Grace*, a track on *Sequel to the Prequel*, Babyshamble's third studio album.

Eternally at odds with commitment, Peter swims this way and that, twists and turns like notes on the breeze. Music was supposed to be a calling, never a career, although necessity has made it such, the songs still carry with them an unkempt glory. Whilst Peter hates leaving home, he follows in the footsteps of his unsettled childhood, moving across Europe, setting up camp, touring, recording, flailing yet triumphant in the grubby bohemian hullabaloo where he always takes centre stage.

Don't be fooled by the glassy far-away eyes, those smashed startled orbs disguise a vast if wilful intellect, his mind a store-house for history, literature, art and music. Few artistes are as timeless in their references as Peter Doherty... or as late: he's the 'king of failed rendez-vous' as one astute if anonymous contributor to the diaries opines.

The diaries, variations of which he's been keeping since he first put pen to paper, came into my possession in the early summer of 2013 but the seeds for this project were planted at least three years earlier, when he was still living in a tiny flat in Kentish Town. He'd not long since come out of prison and seemed a little lost; of course there were plenty of tricks up his sleeve, but nothing particularly tangible. Aside from the prospect of gigs and producing more blood paintings, he briefly touched upon writing. The first volume of his journals, *The Books of Albion,* had been published in a glossy coffee-table format by Orion in 2007 and then reprinted in 2009. Though the tome had won design awards and sold adequately, Peter seemed detached from the project, it was old news and he was ready to move on. Besides which, a certain supermodel's legal team had requested the removal of some of the lad's more piquant observations. 'Write something else and I'll help you edit it...' I tentatively suggested. Then he called his dealer to bring round some chicken with Piri-Piri sauce. I could tell the request was causing consternation at the other end of the line. Was Peter talking in code? In that will-o'-the wisp voice of his, Peter reiterated his order; 'No I just want some chicken with Piri-Piri sauce. Yes, of course I'm sure.' He looked faintly exasperated. 'Just chicken, with sauce... nothing else'... 'Well, maybe some chips, then...'.

Doherty-world is not an easy one to figure out, for much like Albion and its imaginary tributaries, there is no map or instructions. As in the domain of any rock star, there is a court-system and a hierarchy to navigate. Though charming, Peter Doherty doesn't take easily to strangers, induction is a slow process. I owe mine to two stalwarts of the camp, one a musician friend of Peter's whom he sometimes refers to as 'The Count' a.k.a Jerome Alexandre, and the other, 'Professoro', real name, Paul Roundhill. Nonetheless, I had something of my own to offer, a recognised history as an author who has specialised in chronicling the misadventures of rock's most gifted if profligate sons. It was the subject of my first and most enduring book, *Johnny Thunders – In Cold Blood*, that had the greatest appeal for Mr Doherty. What appeared to draw Peter's interest above all was the hidden aspect of the cult of Johnny Thunders. As a teenager, Doherty had heard people talking about Johnny, recognised the aspects of an almost devotional sect, a secret society surrounding the guitarist. He liked the idea of delving for knowledge, into the unknown.

Whilst Johnny Thunders possessed an outlaw cachet, Peter Doherty has a far more mainstream presence. Woven into the fabric of contemporary culture, he is a man of many guises: performer, artist, dreamer, jail-bird, rock star, victim, actor, addict, tear-away, victor... and yet not one single description truly encapsulates Doherty. For the fans, he's a free voice, the last son of an imaginary Bohemia, reading poetry in the long grass, painting in Paris, writing songs of finely wrought poignancy long after midnight. An enigma, Peter Doherty is an essentially paradoxical creature. Initially, I mistook him for a social chameleon, perceiving his variable nature as a sign of mutability, until I came to understand it was not by design but inherent to his nature. Doherty is as transient as the phases of the moon.

At the outset, there was talk of reproducing the most recent diaries, which cover 2008-2013, in the style of *The Books of Albion*. However, although the newer journals follow a similar thread, merging observations with artwork and images, the contents, though rich with character, had become increasingly chaotic and tricky to decipher - a consequence of drug misuse and going days at a time without sleep. When I asked Peter why it was so hard to rest, he replied like a child on Christmas Eve... 'Because there's too much going on.' The substance of the giddy tornado of his mind now romps across the pages that follow.

Adhering to Peter's request, I set about transcribing the most legible and astute strands of the journals. Gradually, a story of sorts broke through the blood, ink and scribbles; a narrative that would lead from his crumbling country pile, Sturmey, to Kentish Town and finally to an apartment in Paris, accompanied by the ballerinas, Céline and Octavie. This was the backbeat to his adventures. The unfolding horror-show is in the often abstract musings upon the extent of his own addiction, not to mention an aborted stay at Thai rehab clinic, Chiang Mai, and his efforts to recuperate afterwards. And yet despite all the bloody junctures, the boy retains a sense of wit and eloquence as he slips in and out of waking dreams, the ebbing and flowing of consciousness; reminiscent of Samuel Taylor Coleridge, another opiate imbiber, who described how, 'The poet's eye in his tipsy hour/ Hath a magnifying power/ Or rather emancipates his eyes/ Of the accidents of size/ In unctuous cone of kindling coal/ Or smoke from his pipe's bole/ His eyes can see phantoms of sublimity.'

Despite Coleridge's fleeting, lyrical genius however, it is another poet that this book is indebted to, namely Arthur Rimbaud. The first time I visited Peter Doherty in Sturmey, I noticed in the careless splendor and squalor, a first edition copy of Verlaine's poetry, amidst a pile of papers and crayons on the floor. It looked as if it had been thrown with the same vigour that Rimbaud might have applied to it during a quarrel with his creative mentor/lover. I shan't use any obvious parallels linking Peter to Rimbaud, suggesting that they both kicked sand in the eye of the establishment, were wild and profligate youths who created a new form of poetic language and challenged society at all turns. But it is no accident that when I returned the journals to Peter in November 2013, he suggested visiting the Rimbaud museum. Though nothing is obvious in Doherty-world, it seemed natural that the latest edition of the journals should follow, as you find it here, in the manner of a Rimbaud-style pocket book.

Nina Antonia April, 2014

Come to Shangri-La to Arcady!

© Nina Antonia 2013

Peter and typewriter, rue de Copenhague, Paris

Editor's Acknowledgements

Thank you to Susan de Muth for her vision and creative empathy.

List of Characters (alphabetical order)

Astile – Peter's son

Allison, Dot – Singer-songwriter, musical collaborator

Anchassi, Sally – Former assistant

Barât, Carl – Former Libertine

Billy Bilo, Bilo Burr, Pipie O'Shea – Peter's alter-egos; they are often the ones to prompt bad behaviour

Boyd, Andy – Co-Manager

Céline Cipolat – Ballerina & former companion

Civil, Blake Fielder – Former husband of Amy Winehouse

Coxon, Graham – Blur/ Doherty musical collaborator

deVidas, Katia – Film-maker, companion

Doherty, AmyJo – Peter's Sister

Escure, Octavie – Ballerina

Elspeth – Former companion

Falkner, Adam – Drummer, Babyshambles

Ficek, Adam – Former drummer, Babyshambles

Gainsbourg, Charlotte – Actor, co-star in *Confessions of a Child of the Century*.

Geldof, Peaches (1989-2014) – Journalist, mother, model, musician

Hunter, Adrian – Manager

Martin, Suze – Singer-songwriter & proprietor of the Doherty/Martin gallery

Mavers, Lee – singer/songwriter, The La's

McCloy, Anne – Multi-media artist

McConnell, Drew – Bassist, Babyshambles

Meurisse, Alize – Writer & artist

Mills, Clara Louise – Friend

Moorish, Lisa – Singer, mother of Peter's son, Astile, & Molly Gallagher

Plinth, Agatha – Confidante

Patterson, Kenny – Road Crew

Professor, the a.k.a Professoro a.k.a Paul Roundhill – Photographer, video-maker, creative catalyst

Roddy, Nadine – former companion

Slater, Iain – Sound engineer

Street, Stephen - Producer

Verheyde, Sylvie – Director *Confessions of a Child of the Century.*

Wass, Alan – Musician.

Whitnall, Mick – Guitarist, Babyshambles

Winehouse, Amy (1983- 2011) – Singer-Songwriter

Wolfe, Peter a.k.a Wolfman - Poet and musician

faith ↗   ↓hope   ↓love

Publisher's Note

Peter Doherty is in the habit of leaving his journals open for friends and visitors to add their own entries. We've indicated when an entry is in a hand other than Peter's by using bold italics; where it is signed by the writer, or otherwise attributed, we have indicated whose it is.

The journals are not strictly chronological with entries sometimes months or even years apart. We have endeavoured to arrange the selected entries along some kind of timeline.

Susan de Muth

2008

In the cab.

'Er, wot do you do?'

Play guitar in a band

'Oh yeah, anyone famous?'

Ha Ha Ha

Well, er I dunno if you'd say famous

More infamous

'Why, who do dya play 4?'

Er, BabyShambles.

Paris somehow brought us crashing down on the cruel side of the wave. Madrid and Barcelona took us heavenwards upon heavenly ledges of foam...

Why would anyone go to all that trouble though, I ask now calm and with legible scribe and clearish thought? The truth is I can convince myself that others are to blame for my tears and yet when the kids are fucked off, these things I can't just brush off...

Tonight's show at Olympia left me broken and empty and deeply paranoid about not only the people around the band but (sinisterly) the band itself. How can this be? After such unity, and aye bonhomie, I am once more crushed and defeated and utterly alone.

Oddly enough, I am back at the hotel with Stef of original 'Alize and Stephanie' fame. Their friendship disintegrated quicker than you can say 'Pete + Carl' a couple of years ago, after hemlock (possibly) escorted the pair of them aboard the good ship Albion one oblivion-dashed New Years Eve.

She is delightful to behold and (can we whisper this) I long to hold and upon her be. Lille of course was the setting for Mik's latest in an unbroken run of bumfests. At one point it was a 'Bakerloo' merry go round bonanza in the confined delirium of the sauna at l'hotel du flap

………….. Remember Hilary in the *Rising Damp* episode in which the aforementioned thespian is auditioning and subsequently rehearsing the other tenants' self-penned play? At one point, a line by Alan (Richard Beckinsale): 'Life's a sham, a lousy hollow sham'. I may have the characters muddled but that's the like analysis and somehow befitting my current gloomy mood.

Awake with a start, a dream, battling it out, conscious of dad's approval? And then trying to push Emily away & mum thinking I was dragging her somewhere.

Ah but Billy Bilo it took you 3 weeks to answer your fucking phone. Prang mixed with the extremely pleasant feeling that comes with splendid isolation. Love it when there are no engagements, gigs, responsibilities, anything. Only the blank covers of the morning, evening, afternoon.

Thank you for coming to Bonn. Today is the happiest day of my life. You're amazing...

This is Daniel - Feelin' tired. A new flame of mind. I've been spending a lot of time with Pete and mates drinking all night at the moment am stoned fuckin hell mate, still getting drunk, sipping cocktails with Pete. My heads all over can't focus!!! Need to stay focused.

On the out 25th March, 2008

And it's Blake C.F, F.C Blake FC

the finest Big House bod D-wings ever seen…

I hope you don't mind me inking this heartfelt shite…

regards, thoughts, gestures, tatty old suits and hats.

I'm at your missus's new gaff by Camden Road over am I.

Hopefully she'll give you this letter this week during the visit.

I hadn't seen Amy for…

That being an aborted mid-flight letter to old Blakester.

A 6-hour drive to Köln and my mother tells me at 5 a.m. that I cannot go 'home' as they are based in army barracks – and so the good lord interferes and plonks the Intercontinental Hotel before me. The same place I stayed with the Shambles shortly after losing this very journal in Barcelona earlier this year. The manageress was tense to say the least and I do not blame her one wit. Our conduct in this historic city was barbaric. Pillaging somewhat & funny.

Get everything working properly

Find the best musicians

Après le smoke, fume?

The submarine nib

Ooh I feel quite overcome.

Conditions of doing as she would do with her 'pleasuring' ting a ting a written oath not to die:

I solemnly swear I am not going to die –

Peaches Geldof

And a day at Ms Moorish's with the youngish. Watching *Fools & Horses* and *Dr Who*. Seeing him more than ever now… and something stirs in me deep inside when we lie on the sofa together watching the Tele. I used to love doing that with my dad. When I was 3 years old or so. Watching *Grandstand* on a Saturday afternoon when he was back off night-shift.

Condemnation from our fathers

Damnation from our lord

But congratulations from our children…

Messrs Doherty and Boyd coping (ha!) with the post-promo and album scoot about (been there, sold the t-shirt) and oblige the Danish beckoning (uhuh) as ever... après gig, only for the Boydster to bring a dozen Scandinavian saucepots back to room 1902 of the 20-storey Radisson Royal near the meat packing district (really, grow up) of Copenhagen. The morning presented thousands of £'s worth of damage and aye, to be sure, not to be seen as 'notching up' girls on the fabled bed-post, perhaps damage to the heart of a (wait for it) blue-eyed, blush-cheeked divinity called... oh does it matter. S'not like I was wasnae more than loving to the girl. And 'girl' at 19 is the opportune (?) word. My blessed lord, at the age of 30, I am now deeming it of interest to note a lover's age.

If I can't vote for Broon it's got to be Boydy

and the guts squirm and gargle with innumerable gasses and gosh the inconvenience of morning has blackmailed me and now I must pretend my skin is not ripped and raw and really not right

on screen charades: a Hollywood beauty who had her fat neck forever hidden by edits and lights that hid it and so dreams come true for dreamers

at least now I'm not wounded but dead

don't look at me like that, for all your practice you make a rotten enemy

once upon a time all that debris would to me have seemed the scenery of fantasy. Faded flags and vintage leather bags. Soggy tenners and dog-eared letters in fawning pigeon English from amateur Italian sleuths remarking on the uncanny similarity between the lyrics to one of my better songs and an obscure Emily Dickinson poem

the night is cold as I uncurl and stretch and arise, it has the drab atmosphere of a long forgotten bomb-site in a long forgotten part of town. This is my room, my dust and my gloom.

Beyond fantasy, without fear

Humiliation & anguish &

Loneliness he caused

Wilful & searching

Never done betray them

If they beg

then it follows you don't wanna be my friend for long...

So how do you make it easy to deliver?

Clever soul that Columbo –

Feigning a dull innocence

Ignorance – interested in trivial confusions

Actually he's a bloody genius

on his knees in the trash can

looking for a clothes label

Pink Tower, Homerton

Who remembers the gates of hell, glass put through to ground by the wild winds of East London. The Wolfman in his night shirt and tracksuit bottoms aghast in opiate-barren agonies as the top half of the flat is open... gutted by the mighty swirling winds of destruction. The bobby's didn't even knock that next morning, one look and they took off.

I'm a lonely man in a dream
Splattered with drops of
Nightmares………..

How long you'll play the hoodlum? Rolling through Hackney with a gun.

Fleecing, grabbing, stooping, scooping, Cagney on the run.

When you're in the gutters
looking up Nothings going to stop us,

no devil man or god no van load of coppers.

I'm hip as hell & the early day's release – filmed behind bars.

All the violence
Her heart can't cope
But nor can her pride
So she smiles
And sings
And sighs secret hopes
that one dark night, she'll swing with the rope,
Swing with the rope,
That one dark night, she'll swing with the rope.

When suffering so we roll into annihilation.

Everyone needs a friend.

The phone is never answered

The keys are never found

The day is never seized

The round is never squared…

For one by nature sensitive it is curious, though mostly unpleasant, to experience the numb blankness that blankets the soul in the midst of a true and keenly attached term of chronic narcotic submersion. The dry fur in the close of the throat, the oily smudged appearance of the mouth and eyes, the stiff back of legs, the swollen and severed arms. The heaving chest. The stained hands and filthy aura. Bombed out mouth and crippled colourless tongue. The vacant opinion and vacuous state of personality. The unpredictable libido and surreal sense of time and space. The psychosis and the blood-letting, head that hangs so heavy around the dark doorway, smoking, ever the... drifting for the eternally... luminous piss and clotted spunk. Sleep at such a strange angle you wake with a hump. All we can hear, the click of lighters, the smack fluffy fizz of scratched records, marvelous soundscapes.

When * walked in I had my cock in a pink mouth and a black finger up my arse. The record was stuck on the word 'never' 'neh-ever' again with an accordion swell behind it on the needle's scratchy return.

I can't stand it any more

I love you

All my awful disgrace

The rowdiness

I mistook for life

... a wild mind, unblessed

Cannonball Adderley shouting out melodic coils alongside the shudda shugga shudda of the drums. This is film score Adderley, pomp and sweeping good feeling. Columbo on a roll. Audrey Hepburn playing in Rome or Paris. Two lovers kissing for the second time. I'll sip Connemara and coke to that!

I prance awhile, sucking on a barrel before the mirror in the main room. Fake playing the old Johanna, flapping my hat out of time. My feet at sixes and sevens. Rasping my tongue along my lips stubble like so many painful bum notes. A swelling of gaseous notes in my throat exalted in a long, indolent belp. Belp! That old one.

Take another look

Another look at the paper

Hide behind the door

Your poor head can't take this any more

What heartache to be found in a son that calls you by his mother's boyfriend's name. Who to resent? Heaven knows it's a choker. Choke 'em both!! Anger subsides seeing the nanny splashing about in a bikini.

Been on my mind of late

Dear K***

Tither and hither

I've half a mind to

Sweep her up

In my arms

For all eternity

Arcady

Last of the English Roses

Salome

New love grows on trees

Lady don't fall backward

1939 Returning

Sweet by & by

A Little Death Around The Eyes

Sheepskin Tearaway

Through the Looking Glass

Broken Love Song

Palace of Bone

29 March 2009. Last night of the tour (save for a rescheduled Grimsby), and a waking dream of an ending to a mostly triumphant meander about France and Albion's provinces. The 'Troxy' in Limehouse was the perfect setting – preserved Art Deco dance hall and balcony luxuriant – for an all-star cast of Arcadian troopers. The full album character play list – Dot, John, Graham, even Stephen Street playing acoustic. We emerged from the shadows and did a turn. String section, Adam, Drew, Mik. But Lee Mavers… as I live and breathe… gracing the wasteland of my shambolic stage. In my heart, in my mind, an era defined. Many demons defied.

Please excuse my English but as Hungarian is my first language... I hope you will understand me!

Thank you for having me today and tonight, for introducing me to Tony Hancock and the sinking stone song!

And for letting me be your designated driver.

I think we had some serious moments amongst the cat shit, the incoherent ramblings and the beautiful stories.

Good Luck tomorrow DXXX

And so I turn my phone on again after some 6 weeks of unsettling summer debacles, deep gut rot and dosh-desperate across the European festival circuit, Latvia, Glasto, Ireland, Scotland, Switzerland, Sweden, Spain, France. I'm mid-curfew, awaiting the leniency or lash of the British justice system.

    Songs of the sea

    Cast into the flames

    False profits tormented

    Forever & ever

Freezing lost to melt and knowing you're awaiting the well-known torment. In the shadows watching the flies spiraling in the warm drafts. Here comes the night with a brick in its hand, staving in people's minds.

Melody soothes and releases like a wrist and a fist. May the night never end and now is ready for that sombre, breathless sorrow sends. Buck their trends and fuck their bends. When you think there's no escape from the sunken dream wishing you could swim, wishing you were belly pot thin. Understand the sodding see-saw makes sorrow so silly when you're swinging and singing. Freedom's not fucking about, savour it.

And the tannoy-blessed Eurostar pulls out of Gare du Nord, and the Shambles contingent are Blighty-bound for a week's respite before resuming the tour in Deutschland
    Deutschland
    Deutschland
    Deutschland
    Today I am hot-footing it on arrival straight to West London magistrates for the latest in my regular reviews of my probation
    Superior requirements
    My next drug testing in Sainsbury shouldn't be too far away
    Approaching the outskirts of Paris and 'gay' it certainly does not fit the description - unless overcast, grey and chilly be 'gay' in these times of fast evolving language

And so the long hard slog has had the Shambles machine turn its final cog and I return to Sturmey via probation this dark, clear Wiltshire night.

The cats are unusually interested in my movements and I am sad to report nameless grey kitten had died of cat fever.

    There's like, no home place
    There's no place like home

In this startled state, within the hollow silence of the ever so early morning, every noise is so significant, a series of innocent sounds will now become an intricate conspiracy...

Ever the amiable host

Of trouble and strife

Most run for their life

I do like a bit of gingham

and the fire burns, spitting and crackling like the devil's business. I'm at Lisa's with Astile, Molly and Chelsea the pregnant cat. She's already huge 5 or 6 babies in there I'd say. I'm setting up an Albion Rooms in her cottage annexe. Old iron bed frame, wooden dresser, small dressing mirror, wooden floors. Jedi knights, Ewoks and death stars.

Any eminent criminal appears to be superior in many respects - superior in initiative, intelligence & originality - to the average judge...

'Twas upon the bottom bunk in the dull-yellow shabbiness of the prison cell that I shared with a quad/motorbike thief.

'Twas there that Radio 4 crackled and fizzed and drew complaints from the top bunk and told the radio play tale of a medieval king and his battles, his queen, his impassioned defence of the Holy Roman Church...

People saying 'bollocks' on Radio 4 rather tickles my fancy. Anglo-saxon oaths.

Narco imperialism, Gun Boats

Burn the summer palaces

The first opium war

The seizure of Hong-Kong

Blood stained fathers,

Desolate mothers

'God made the son for this man'

Napoleon

All the cradles and all the tombs were armed with butchers.

Only corpses and demi-gods.

The blues ain't nothing but a good woman on your mind

And the rat-tat-tat-ta-tattoo

Of the winding run of turnings

That chime with pangs of bone rattling clangs, soak'd to the soul

Lick lip salty

Tears that tear through the blanket of the wild wind

Whip up and woe and woawoh

With yodelay ye you

The only time you feel like crying

And the door caught her frock in its crushed fingers

Wolf blues there grinning…

Seeing the piggy squealing

Flames licking their hides

My true hearted girl

Laid it on the line

Gave me a week

And a week ain't no time

No time to decide

If I want her by my side

She sick and tired

Of me sick or wired

She wants me inspired

Free and alive

So I have to decide

If she stays by my side

Seven days I am given

To make this decision...

Never let anyone be

Unwittingly led astray

But many astray still

German immigrant, shuffling around the front room of a Camden town basement.

'He is my shape, he does whatever I want.'

Ah now I think that told her

(I never will, you know it's true)

My my we got a fine one

Where we go the way'll be -

Random rows of ridiculous rhymes,

Clunking strung-out chimes

Ra-ra we lead from the free

Ah, we do ever after and

What have they done with the dance halls

Take us to another another place

Calling the rest of the Faithful

Pick up the pace & pipe your prayers in time

Nah nah they don't give a monkey's

Running on empty

You'll be surprised how

many miles you can get on this time...

'Hello Spaceboy'

Life being one huge build-up

Waiting for itself to begin

And this end still works

If it doesn't it is not the ending,

but the place the ending was to be...

Bejayzes.

Wobbling off balance down the fuzzy grey aisle of the train. Reach out for a steady arm to keep me from slapstick.

   The carriage is possibly empty. A chain supports me.

   Pipie O'Shea in the small metal kharzi wobbling back.

   K*** is chicly, cheekily, charmingly smiling from the front of *Grazia*. French *Grazia*. My arch-enemies of course.

The gushing 6-page spread and most notable is my complete and annoyingly annoying absence entirely from the positive, polished, PR fantasy biography that is adorned with many a classy snap including one of K***'s gay best mate and successful hairdresser and huntsman 'Leader of the Hunt' if I remember correctly.

   The insult is compounded by photographs of a hundred of her other ex-dildos.

   Dear oh dear… why this? Gets to me so, perhaps a little more than I would care to admit.

   So, my confidential, cardboard covered book of Albion, I am still in love with the woman with the girl.

The ecstasies that I suffered and the time that we passed in each other's arms were of such import and revelation to any heart that I shall never truly feel any different than I did that first day in the barn, in the old barn...

I prefer to die for my ideas

Than dying, suffering, in my bed.

To distinguish between life and death. But the two are beautiful.

Fine: what atrocities this good morrow? What is indeed to be done at last...

A slug of fresh water

A romantic thought

– this tiny room – shadows of passing cars, a sleeping girl's hand…

Delirious and demented.

When the heebees met the jeebees it was hoo-rah............
Never the twain should meet again

Look what they done to the boy

Did the unthinkable
Sunk the unsinkable.

Gangster shot his pal today
As they took him in I heard him say

Diddy wah diddy
Diddy wah diddy

I just found out what diddy wah diddy means…

Somethings from thineself

only one self

can submerge the truth of matters, the heart of matters being

oft times recorded for all posterity and future perusal

All not always is lost forever

(thin knees up to his nose, clay pipe jutting out of mouth – A

three pipe problem)

And Wolfe stumbles across Passport control, into the arena of

the international jet-setters.

Under the watchful eye of the luminous policeman he sits

next to me on the padded bench.

'And now we're here' he concurs.

Tells murky tales of flea-infested dogs calmed by Diazepam.

These days – sans dramas, sans schedules, sans funds but over something wonderful and why – so close to happiness.

Audio book, the crannies and nooks of that heaving heart Predominantly in my heart are contemplative courses of tumult.

C'est Vrai?

Doubt feeling... imperceptible... that the sun may never shine or that bed-clothes will not crease but do not doubt my debate with that most variable of constants – the date, the damned and dashed date. How the fuck (pardon my French) is it 31st October already? Tell me that...

Fuck knows anyhow, I'm all dissolved in my post implant sobbings, peeing and furtive and full of the squirts. Aye they'll pass.

Help, I need somebody, anybody............

Copped for all I wanted

Copped for all I wanted

Forgot what I needed

Lost all I had – you know dignity, integrity, responsibility

Men like you

Can't learn anything from men like me

But we come from men like you

By and large taking everything into account, all things considered you have me as you had my secretary, your way over the barrel… once again the lad himself fell prey to the malicious scheming of his old pal * . This the lynch pin, the apple core, the central theme of themes.

My life's one constant… do I do myself wrong to give in?

I will be found a stranger in my own skin,
wonder how I ever let me in.

⁂

Awaken to an empty house. Have a mooch about. I tink it's a Sunday. 'Tis wintry outside this Autumn. Electric and phone situation fucked but 'tis warmish. Listen to a bit of the Who, James Brown, have a hot bath. Vix vapo rub. Go looking for crumbs.

No guard at all.

Criminal, insane, sensation. Cobblers mate.

Apple-gobbled pig-headed on a plate.

Oh go on give over, you love a new nib.

And immortal strains

mournfully

melancholy

make their way from the hall.

It's the Beatles, 'If I Fell'.

'When she learns that we are twoooo'.

Blow & Mo's testimony
Cannon St Massive.
Thug life Gun shooting nation
If anyone fuck with P, Mo & Blow is there
Fuck all of ya.

'God save the King' say all the old flags and banners. And they'll have their day again but naturally. The house phone rings. It's A or G perhaps. He reckons 40 minutes. So that'll be a what? A 3 day blank? What a dreary, uninspiring night, the night of the crack-head. Heart's flame. Cats purr steadily, always. Solitary passing cars always seem to stop in the dead of night here. A bath wouldn't go amiss.

Ah that wasn't being very nice was it? Telling her that... arranging something else, I'll be straight. I'm not a rotten man, but try and catch the wind before you go without hurting someone.

Wells me up tear- like.

Oh C...

You're made to dance with me, should come with me

Let's dance and sing our lives and see
What becomes of the whole dream

Dance and sing our lives away
Dance and sing our lives away

Trust me to go and fall for a gangster's daughter

Caught a sort of half-evil reference to a

Bloke he'd caught

Upsetting his daughter

He lost 6 & ¼ pints of bad red blood

Now every couple has their ups and downs

I'll grant ya, and tempers can get heated

One little push, it left her seated

He had me carried over in the trunk of me old Rover

He said did you slap my baby?

I said 'Sir what was to be done?

She'd smashed up my best guitars

Laptops, clothes and cars'

And he thought hard and long

Listening to a Sinatra song

He picked up a nine iron club

And said 'Fancy a few rounds?'

Oh boys I warn you

Beware legs in denim shorts yeah

If they're a hoodlum's daughter

You may find you wind up

All tied up and tortured

Lamb to the Slaughter

All she got was a sore lip

I nearly got fed to the pigs.

I've half a mind to ramble on

About you being 21

Silly? Untold birthday songs

Sing them all day long

Linger on your eyes

Your elegance invites

Yeah, your divine dancing eyes

And how they're green in moonlit skies

Oh I could warn you birthday girl

Of the strange and dangerous world

I'm crouching in one sock

Defying all the clocks

You tip the poison out the bed

And turn my white sheets red

But the poison in my head, it'll start

To trickle from heart to heart

As we lay there arm in arm

I'm sounding the alarm

Get out while you can my love

I'm a solitary man

Lonely, lost of soul

Take this love affair we've had

I cherish it

But I feel it counting up

Counting down, somewhere…

Ah, distant friend, virtually strangers now.

I have betrayed you, fail oneself in my promise to unite, to describe to survive amongst these pages.

We were betrothed for you to exist, P must insist to apply my thoughts, my worries, my queries, a horizon this landscape of parchment. To while away the hours, to add fuel to our fires but I ain't the 'Scribe' squire. I'm just living life, put that in your pipe and smoke it*.

*Entry by Nadine Roddy

So that won't move you, not in the immediate climate of your clouded clout. You can't stay forever and it wouldn't be nice anyway...

(a short journey later)

Infernal whining, whine of some distemper – photo input cable.

All that's missing is the dodger's Gibson and a huge rock of ages or three, yesterday. I thought ever so briefly before crashing that the chaps from Chatham might have half-inched the geetar and even had half a mind o' day dream about going after them, retrieving my baby... Perhaps it'll turn up, eh? Yeah once my brain has neutralised while I have a shufty about.

So, to do list:

Get dressed

Songs

Paris

Find lost guitar

Find lost rock

Tidy Bedroom

Stop the whine

See if Mik's upstairs

Socket

Adaptor

Was it really hell I dreamt of? Partially hellish dream and other slumbers, some band, the next generation on from The Paddingtons was showing me around town as I'd rolled up lost in some rusty bus. They were most hospitable and excited when their new record was being reviewed in the NME. Ended up on the town in, Hull? Liverpool? Now hailing a cab. Ferocious dream no? It's all go in this lad's subconscious.

Del and Rodders

Flipped up and at an angle; the sirens flashing and white in the oily inky blue.

The red tops were alleging that Amy and I were at it like rabid nymphomaniac dogs.

The plot thickens... safe in the knowledge that that night was a... I was honestly able to defend myself, and sadly shook my head in pity and sadness that Blakey should even for a second doubt my loyalty.

Now then... after they divorced I still hadn't even dreamed of upon the Winehouse making a move and yet it seemed that Blake was still threatening all manner of unspeakable acts upon my head, convinced as he was that I'd doinked his dearest ex-missus. Streuth! Now then at some point of course, particularly just after stage at V-Festival last year I had a too brief a jig of Humpty Dumpty with the Duchess and it all comes to a head now that they appear to be seeing each other again. He's texting me thinly-veiled threats in his suitable state. Could turn nasty, nasty, nasty. Giving some big-house slag a back hander – probably two pence to bash me about like a plastic inflatable horses head. Possibly.

The Grandstand theme plays as the toddler piles on top of his uniformed father, sleeping, stretched out on the sofa, just back from the nightshift in the guards room of the barracks. In the small front room of 111, Mountview Drive, County Antrim, an end of terrace house on a steep hill, overlooking much of Lisburn and the surrounding hills, dark and forbidding on the horizon.

'I'll fight any man in here!'

Then his pet mouse pops up from the jacket pocket. Downs a whisky,

belches,

mouse parp (sounds like car starting)

and says

'I'll fight any cat here...'

Dear Peter - Thanks for putting me up – I've gone to check out possible accommodation at Dock St in E1. Gissa job!

Xxxx

What was she arrested for? Attending a flight assaultant.

The taxi's waiting. There's blood on this phone.

entry is a random, barely legible clutter of sick and sodden sorrows from some sunken souls scribbled scraps of some sort of self-styled services of statements, stories, songs and strangeness, some secrets and silliness. Silliness?
Sillyness……..

Peter – Nowt is sweeter

I love Stella

String Vest

Wife Beater

Dirty Defeata

Love you

Peter

Forever

& Evs

Your

*Amy**

*Message from Amy Winehouse

You were often kissing a lost girl, remembering phony names, statutes of limitations on the main act, wasting my breath when I sing. It once meant the world and now means nothing. He's famous, or will be in a minute.

She's lying. He's too talented to have sex with.

Tis quite constant now, regular even though unpredictable. Often drug related, which surprised me. Something slightly fatal happened in amongst the tuzzling, the charming and the teasing, the pleasantries, amidst all that is the… the unspeakable, the unpronounceable, the improbable, the unpleasant.

I know she is staring at me… I can feel her pretty dark eyes tearing into me, somehow though they pry, they have always been welcome. And since she WILL come, oh but she will…

THE FIGHT BEHIND LOCKED DOORS

Should be a good scrap that one, evenly matched as it is - both sides if you like - notwithstanding your disapproval - being worthy of their respective honoured status in public life. Their celebrity and the saturation levels of media interest & recognition, speculation & celebration, criticism & admiration, persecution & intensity

Peter - versus - The Monkey
ding/ding

Her head slumps forward in the age-old junk nod or the gauch as it is known

Peter I cannot, for I have not heart, it is made of marble.

Even so I do not like to be charmed and tricked so, this being my birthday and all, how bouts you present me with the truth?

Waiting rooms, hoping rooms they should call them.

Shrewd as a shrew... lewd as lube... fun as a funeral.

Brown and gout in Paris and London.

The implant* there, bulging away in the midriff suddenly it seems ill at ease and in the shut-eye dark of recent gauching – on its last lap of this ragged body's blotted trail of tracks and veins.

Beneath the stinging, superficial pain and of late constant pang of bona-fide torment. I was warned by neighbours and baby-mother Ms Moorish, that the chicken was out of date t'other day.

Cramps of some description are turning over in me gut – think my gut is in schtuck anyway.

The phone rings on the far-side of the room, shifting from side to side occasionally, relaying people's pointless attempts to communicate with me.

There's a pattern developing, a resentment slowly builds as the same individuals take great personal offense if you do not answer or get back to them.

---

* Opiate blocking implant inserted into the lower abdomen, intended to help beat heroin addiction.

I make a rare text to a painter of sorts. I say sort, she's actually a sweet, pretty, talented artist. Thin and doe-eyed, young and sunny as a treacle tart with tons of tongue whipping sauce upon it. Not enough to model her looks but then again she's too busy getting her novels published to bother with all that vacuous gloss I s'pose. Anyway, I text her, 'Hello Beautiful'; she replies, 'Bonsoir handsome'.

I respond to a text from her former best friend and now sworn enemy, arranging to meet her at my flat. Strange move. She may be honey and ginger or pineapple and strawberry blonde.

Hypnotist

Today we see Dr Sanchez.

First Sylvie and I come to an arrangement: 1 hit per day and she has 3 fags a day.

Meanwhile in the taxi we head west of central Paris.

A girl in a grey and orange fur sits on the back of a scooter at the lights.

The Galway bar glides past.

A fat man sits on a green metal bench.

You are the enemy of everything that loves.

Do not wait for old age.

Do not leave a child on this earth.

Do not fertilise the corrupt, erase yourself like smoke.

That's not what you told me. Is that because you didn't know? If you didn't know why didn't you tell me? You lied to me, my friend.

Edward G. Robinson, fearful enough as Pete Morgan, the wild-eyed tyrant haunted by murderous screams from the woods.

A cool wind spills in the window of room 221 of the Hotel Meridian, Barcelona.

If you fall from a high enough spot, you die before hitting ground.

Die if you try.

Fuckin' Statement*

To the press, fans and management.

1st n' foremost, Mik n' Pete would like to apologise to those people who witnessed the band's daleance [sic] into a space jazz oddessy at the Charlotte St Blues club.

We want to explain about the reasons behind the recent events. We (Mik n' Pete) want the music we make to be the best it can possibly be. To do this we need people in the band to play and rehearse as much as possible. Also just to be around and be available to play all the time but it's got to the point where we had to book appointments to rehearse and when we did it was for 1-2 hours max. Also it was laboured and awkward. Mik hired a studio for a year and spent £150,000 on recordin' equipment. In the year we had the studio Adam and Drew came three times. Also Pete rented a house with enough room etc for the whole band to move in and live and rehearse. Again in the two years we had the house they came a total of eight times. They may argue that when they have, that no work is ever done but to put it in the words of Mik – 'Adam came down and said, "well I've been here thirty minutes and nothing has happened". Well I'd been there three days and nothing was happening'.

The creative process can't be forced and people have to at least be there to make it happen.

We feel that the music was suffering as a result of the other band members never being there.

The only time we get to play new songs is on stage, which is ridiculous.

Sometimes people get spoilt or looz perspective. There are millions o' people who get up at 6 in the morning and work on building sites for nothing. Not only do they work for nothing they work for a living.

Babyshambles will live forever.

Love you boys! X

* Statement written by Mik Whitnall

Mikkle, gone to the location, left you some money.

Yummy little Californian lawyer

WASP

Light blue skin

Impersonal

Over-cooked apple sauce flavour body odour

Do those American girls exist anymore?

Did they ever exist?

... when is a strong-minded

Soaring soul Irish woman

Gonna come and grab holda me and

Save my soul?

Crash into my arms, see rings of pink flesh, infected pools of torn skin and orange tracks, shouting the snaking routes of so many holy veins by the elbows join, bulbous lumps of hardened tissue decorate the inside of the arms along with thin scabs of black and claret. At once both swollen and saggy – a rare and disgusting combination. The mermaid on the right forearm is guillotined at the tail by long winding tracks marks matched only by the tube map on the left. I will say though that my nails are very clean today.

I must call it 'our bed' for we sleep in it. It must be 'our room' because we wake in it and rake through love all about it and that then 'our love'.

Let it not be a rushed through performance, or a steady, choreographed dance. Let it not be token or trophy or tittle-tattle for the voyeurs. Let it not be heart-washed into fanatical self-sacrifice, ready to blow itself into a million little pieces on a promise of an eternity of infinite splendor and legend and box ticked agendas completed and filed under 'intensity of love'.

I had asked her how her love-life was, and then tried to retract the question.

She says she now has difficulties in that she compares everyone to him and they have thus far failed to inspire her, or match up to a comparable requirement.

She is beautiful, and in the dull light of Saint-Germain-des-Prés her hair is blonde, now golden, and under the red light of a large bulb, it is soft rouge. She nibbles a croissant. I pull her to me and feel old-fashioned as I kiss her hand.

People are not afraid of suffocation because they can justify it with the control of sexuality. Maybe it's that I try to understand.

Sucking endlessly on the pipe, this one a gold-coloured metal affair.

Trying to come to terms with the Parisian night.

The * * saga rolls on for the best part of the week. It has caused much to-do and much ado and ended now with me crossing Paris at 2 a.m. to meet the so-called model and actress, only to literally do a runner, fleeing, as I did from the confused lady in black leather trousers

The French man doesn't always run away.

Napoleon seemed largely unbeatable.

Couldn't crack the British though, even with the blockade on British trade.

'Soldiers of General Ludd'...

'Enoch'

'Luddites.

'Breaking machines.'

1815 – Wellington beat Napoleon at Waterloo.

You made a powder keg out of your head and a sand trap of your bed. Your pockets are packed with rockets of smack and that is all there is to be said.

> Mr Myrtle hit rock bottom
> Now unsung and long forgotten
> His name is lost in fact it's rotten…
> Poor old Myrtly Moo.

Found to be a little close to home
When you're left with gaping holes
When the sound of rattling bones
Stops anyone from dreaming at night.

Hmmm, my memory is potted of late. I have been a tad concerned by one or two decidedly elementary errors.

Indeed last night I awoke in the evening after having a dream that involved a nightmarish twist whereby I couldn't remember the door code to my own home in rue de Copenhague.

I was awoken by Adrian phoning from the street wanting to come in.

To my bemusement and awe, horror – I could not remember the 5-digit code in reality either.

It is now 6.11 on the Saturday morning following the concert at Le Gibus.

Zap, Kalopsh, Bifpowzapp!

Paris, I fancy – I muse, this hour of pre-enlightenment – never fails to get one these dramatic outbursts of gushing gratitude.

Normally the stock opening to the soliloquy is: 'Paris never fails to live and die up to beyond exquisite expectations…'

From the velvet prang fuck soul squishing of Le Tigre (the ex-pole dancing club where I played a wee acoustic set this night past) to the bright, clean and spacious apartment in rue de Copenhague, the rooms that the Ballerinas and I have taken…

'La Guerre de Loisirs' in the rue de Copenhague kitchen.

Céline pads about the apartment.

'Are you hungry?' she asks.

'No'.

'Are you angry?' she asks.

Treading carefully, quietly, about the apartment. The whole city is dead or asleep, and then I hear a cough from the bedroom...

This here book [journal] would've been a *bona-fide* treat for AmyJo and myself when we were kids. We would spend hours playing a game with dolls or perhaps cards.

We were quite old-fashioned kids in many respects. Kind of sweet, thinking of it now, the both of us in our Naafi clobber playing our intricately plotted games with a whole host of characters that we each played – football hooligans, fat ladies, scousers, cockneys, Germans, people that we thought the world was made up off.

Enormous comic weight was carried by each and every one of them in our eyes anyway we would record our sketches on tapes and, in the later years, on a home movie camera when technology progressed. I seem to remember dad borrowing one from work as the phrase went...

For whom it tolls in rousing song

To pull you to me from the throng.

I watch for you night and day.

Come to Shangri-la to Arcady!

He saw her eyes and surmised

He'd forever be on a loop of 'Woe is me'

The type of gloop he so despised.

You and me are sloths

It's not all my fault

You and I are 1

You and I are slowly

Rolling into one single slot

Nobody's fault – Pinkman and Walt

Jekyll and Hyde

Everybody sighed – Bonny and Clyde

You and me I'm not sorry to say are riding a trolley

Through some sorry states.

Was re-watching Edward G Robinson in 'Scarlet Street'

'Oh please kitten....'

'For Pete's sake………..'

Promoted beyond his gifts

By the spirit of the age

Bloated, blotto, shit

Swollen, scabby mange...

He's given up on his poetry

'You're talking human again'

'Sorry?'

'You don't have to be sorry, it's good to talk in different ways.'

Every sound is amplified in this atmosphere.
The flame candles lick at, matches at.
The shady darkness.
My eyes feel glazed and wider.

It keeps close the shadows that so free become when the darkness that binds them melts in the sun.

It holds fast the spirit of laughter and song
When it gets dragged asunder in murderous throng and likewise
The sadness and sorrow it binds to our life.

When the slang-using junky decided to concentrate on his writing of music and cut down on junk, it was a case of putting the art before the horse.

There's only so much they can say about Junk, Moss, dirt and dishonour before their snide is on repeat. Redundant. At which point, looks replace tuts, which in turn replace the snide & smut that clings flimsy like soot on skin.

I put words into the gaps that nonsensical shouts

Leave between the slopes

Of traffic, slopes and sloping off roars

Sounds gradually rising and then falling away

It's terrifying what I imagine really

Decreasingly so, though

Anyways… who is this that that I live with now?

A girl that I have always loved

All this plays out and

She lies silent and still

And the nonsense continues.

This entire thing is causing me no little end of strife

See I want her to want her claws in me

This girl who is of life

I crashed into your life

And you tip-toed away

Out of sight

Chère M****, and so we meet again... one whole year has passed since our last encounter, a brief rendezvous backstage at some festival or other... I have the vaguest sensation that we were not on the best of terms that day. In fact, we have not been 'cosy' - if you see what I mean -for a great deal longer than a year now... some sensational revelation is at hand, aye!

My heart was but suddenly filled with the ecstatic joy that can only come from being in love... I had the most exhilarating rush to know that you existed.

Swiftly on the coat-tails of this glorious burst of love was the tragic counterpoint; the certainty that my love for you had come somewhat too late... you had long since given up on our love affair.

I was blind to your declarations and displays of loyalty and devotion. I was deaf, dumb and numb to your sweet, sweet soul's love.

'Eee by gum, what had I gone and done?'

'You are beautiful, precious...'

Edward G. Robinson's racketeer mobster is well narked off that Kid Galahad has been 'sparring' (ahem) with his refined and molly-coddled sister.

The truth is that the sister wants to have a good time and resents her brother's protective - and, to her eyes, hypocritical - way of bringing her up. He's involved in the thriving Miami underworld of wise-guys and loose women and yet she is expected to stay at home in a quiet country environment. She wants to go out, have a right ol' knees up, and subsequently falls arse over tit for 'Kid Galahad' her brother's newest heavyweight contender and so called because of his chivalrous response to some hoodlum's behaviour towards ladies at a party where he was then a waiter or 'bell-hop' for it was a hotel.

Anyway, on his deathbed at the end, Edward G. Robinson's character repents: 'I was wrong about the Kid,' he says to his sister. 'Seems I was wrong about a lot of things.'

Indigenous rainforest communities simply ploughed through, dispersed, desecrated and depleted – in short, dealt with – for logging, you understand.

Evidently Jerome Lewis, a lecturer in anthropology at University College London, has devised a method of clocking – via GPS satellite – their areas of land, their homes and hunting grounds, sacred places.

Communities are those best able to prevent the seemingly unstoppable tidal wave of ecological decimation.

For Chris-sakes I remember learning about the depletion of the rainforest whilst I was at primary school, 1985, 1986, 20 odd years ago... I remember sitting at primary school, cold, high ceiling, stone ex-farmhouse classroom, sat there agog as I computed the knowledge that an area the size of a football pitch was being destroyed every second.

'EEZEE Bruv...' a pin-dimpled, scraggy, round pink face, all a-fleck with white flakes of skin, comes too close for comfort in the wash of the light spring air.

Something isn't snapping... the big-faced oddity seems to be keen on ruining me in some manner or another, but there's a fault in his mechanism.

He's grinning most worryingly, close and annoyingly, but it's like I'm on ice, and float off and away with me pot of porridge and juice from Pret a Manger.

Is he confused in my memory with the trampish bod outside McDonald's?

No less threatening but insists that he needs 72p.

Let me not to the marriage of two minds

Admit impediments. Love is not love

Which alters when it alteration finds,

Or bends with the remover to remove

Oh no! it is an ever-fixed mark

That looks on tempests and is never shaken;

It is the star to every wandering bark,

Whose worth's unknown, although his height be taken.

Love's not Time's fool, though rosy lips and cheeks within his

bending sickle's compass come;

Love alters not with his brief hours and weeks,

But bears it out even to the edge of doom.

If this be error and upon me proved

I never writ, nor no man ever loved.

(Shakespeare, Sonnet 116)

Cursed is he who will disclose

The converse held beneath the rose

When friend meets friend

Subtle the sign

And toast it well

In ale or wine

The world may seek to pry within

May swear you do a social sin

But shun them for their taunts and jeers

And hate them for their itching ears!

Believe me it is heaven to blend

In faith with a familiar friend

Distorted thinking

Turns into toxic feeling

Which turns into

Slippery behaviour

'We got the goods on you...'

I attempted to be mad at 'Nstein – asked him what on earth he was doing terrifying young girls by falling about violently, naked, abusive, pissing on the bed of absurdities...

He laughed in a slurred, cackly, moan,

'Eh? You taught me that one, that's what you do...'

I couldn't argue with him.

I remember the infamous Pink Tower lampissing incident.

Tried to kill myself as a birthday treat for 'Nstein by using a lash of piss as an electricity conductor but only succeeded in short-circuiting the whole house.

The golem slips from the bed and pads with blood-mauling plates of meat about his Pandemonia...

Such solemn steps on the orange strips flooding the dark flat...

All about is Pandemonia

Such a solemn golem startled with his massive drug habit that brings about total derangement

'To make it good, you must break bad' – whatever the hell that actually means...

Me old son – you're so much better off getting you know what –

A shot…

Same feeling, kept on the low boil, spaces between breaths, slight silence between shadows silently scampering up the walls.

The world's asleep,

deep in pre-paid dreams,

moronic spasmodic screams

and the rat catchers go round in teams

(catratchets)

Playing guitar in a hallway, people gathering, the carpeted chambers, worried about the state of your teeth, fine everlasting choppers and oh the fine everlasting hair.

Cope please cope, someone has to cope

Now then now then what's all the hullaballoo? What's all the to-do..?

What the devil is getting to you... Some pitiful, invisible blockage is preventing you from padding up the stairs, having a shower and rehearsing your trousers?

Well stuff my new boots man, get the fuck!

And so I did... and the vision is complete – long sidelong glance out of the long open window, high up over the alleyway, a mass of ivy leaves all but cover the bricks, all but hide the high Parisian wall, in the slow white glow of après sunrise.

The broken day.

Who has got a little wiggle?

My baby....

Shimmies side to side across the middle?

My baby...

Love it when she feigns kicking me up the backside in the street...

Usually her quick reflex response to some joke about her appearance... some joke! 99 times out of 99 it's a heartfelt compliment lazily dressed up as a derogatory remark.

'I'd love to pretend, but it's clear... I'm falling in love with you my dear.'

And you look at me all wide-eyed and insist that I do this sort of thing all the time...

If I wasn't a gentleman then I'd suggest that if anyone was familiar to this scene, then, well, it's actually her job to 'look after' the young men who play the venue in Kiev where she works with the bands, mostly American or British...

I can imagine the number of flash gits in bands who have tried it on with her. I told her as much... she indignantly expressed her dislike for the boys in bands who did indeed try to seduce her: 'They all say they have girlfriends', as if that was a reason for her to be more likely to go with them. I think that is what she said.

Anyway, by the time I was tentatively testing the water on such matters the pair of us had left the club and were in a posh apartment high above the city. It was very dark. Three days and eight cancelled flights later, I was still in Kiev, marveling at the remarkable and flawless skin that covered her long limbs, and indeed much of the rest of her.

The day unfolds in ever more beautiful chapters.

On the street I am greeted by the lady who I will spend the rest of my incredible life with.

Céline and Octavie receive the most amazing news ever...

and Drew (who we visit at the Royal London Hospital Whitechapel) is declared, 'Free from serious illness or damage' by the doctors.

My first night in my new bed.

Are you still stretching in your bed in Paris?

Shuddering boiler.

Stuttered metallic belches in the old building.

The shame – I shouldered

The pain – I soldiered

The fame – I'm over it

Although the whole lot of you are sold on it

Piled up on all the rot

Reaching for the top

'I want what I want...'

'A few years ago I wanted a rich husband'
'And now?'
'Well, I still do I suppose.'

Pretty, pretty tann'd face
Blonde haired young woman
Tall, cheerful, deeply sad at heart.

We refer to each as brother and sister and not without genuine platonic affection...

Never really fancied her. Don't think she ever fancied me either. Rich husband indeed!

You do insist on putting yourself in that position.
You should resist thyself and all your trappings
these hard earned freedoms
that you have cleverly crafted into a whole cycle of
clampdowns on reality.

There is a tranquility in the apartment now.
My room is glowing in the fuzzy, candle-lit shadows of post intensive tidy energy – from an uber-stylish furniture shop near Bastille got a quartet of rackety old bureaucratic filing cabinets. Tall, slender and grey, they match 2 that I bought previously from the brocante…

Strangely I'm keeping the room in good order… in the silk smoking gown my mum got me, piping ink a good 'un and working on some decidedly accomplished melodies.

I scrawl as ever in the books that clutter my new metal cabinet… but a sound, solid, body of lyrics for songs does not come.

The furious desire I used to have, channeling my every nerve, every fantasy, every fear into songs.

Staging my fantasy role plays for the 'fame game' freak show that I self-perpetuated, music, emotion, manipulation.

The crinkle of the foil

The sprinkle of the sandy soil

The twinkling of the eyes

The pupils who decrease in size.

A rush of sequences flashes of dull psychotic crashes

Ears pops and stab and flush

The jawline wreaks havoc

On the tombstone teeth

The head spins in dizzy momentary deafness

Still her voice, steady and calm, level and

Somehow both low and loud,

Low tones of collusion and pronounced artifice.

What a wonderful world we have inherited from our forefathers...

for a moment my mind seemed to teeter on the edge of some pitiless canyon just considering the ingenuity, imagination and impossibly creative craftsmanship of mankind through the ages...

for a second, history itself seems a peculiar enough affair all in all the fact we have records of achievements or do we?

Conspiracies, war, evolution, revolution, civilizations, refrigerators, darts, water balloons, electricity, ah the boggling mind, the beautiful soul, the bloody heart.

And so we pick up where we left off, where we always leave off – once upon (or near as dammit) a time exactly like this one. Clammy, elegant, jaw clenches in the throes of melody or disinterested prang.

My black jeans are indeed spattered with dried glossy blood spots and circles. My cheeks have artificial dimples, soiled infinite teeth clamp chatter.

How delightful, this grimy scruff-bag swanning through 'business premier' (of late a bi-weekly excursion) the vaguely luxurious Eurostar class of travel.

Alcohol, coffee, exotic teas and magazines galore. I dug into a soft kiwi and had some wasabi nuts, civilized indeed.

At 32, I do not snaffle bottles of brandy and bang up in the bogs, every journey.

On seeing as how, on being as how, that very notebook is adorned with pencil outlined legs of the 'Crazy Horse' signature, I might lead you, gentle reader, straight through the main thoroughfare of this entry's musing.

I left the 1st floor apartment of rue de Copenhague this evening with a wall behind each eye.

Paris had been lovely enough to me this confusing evening. Was it my manner? My casually pre-judged infidelity and the judgemental…

Anyway (soz I'm nodding off as the train pulls out of Gare Du Nord…)

What the divil was I on about?

Aye... the bad tempered cunts in the photocopying shop, and the mystery of the stolen ribbon.

I only ended up in the gaffe originally to use the princesses' pop-lamp as a prop, for the beautiful Céline's birthday gift (naturellement), but also to allow me to pass back along the edge of my courtyard and along the huge window of a dear neighbour who was entirely divine in black negligee, which was quickly removed to reveal knickers and bra. The girl was seemingly preoccupied talking with another (fully clothed) lass. They were laughing, oblivious, and of course I instantly ran through a mental list of sorts at my lustful disposal in Paris, ah dear, where does it get us? Pining in 'business premier' I shouldn't wonder.

The visit to Crazy Horse was... all dimensions exactly equal. The girls came on in bearskin titfers, gloves, boots and very little else and mimicked the Buckingham Palace guards: hands on shoulders, straight arms, the rigid stature and - to my sheer delight - the reflex spring bounce of the forearm after saluting.

All knockers just about the same size – what you might call 'small' or tiny even or perfect!!!

'Never mind where I tell you to stand. You stand where I tell you.'

I scrubbed up, looked a bit of a character, could be a musician or something in Camden, monitored swallowing meth and some libs for a man of such distinction in the that field. It's like a heart surgeon forced to scrape up road kill. Even if the chemist has a sparkly floor and the Indian girl is real cute and wobbled a bit when I got to the counter and removed my hat.

And a wee snooze, including the gruntingly belch-groan that would rouse me just as I would nod off, and drew quizzical queer looks from the young Irish lady I was sharing the two-seater table with. And, oh really, have I had to come to London just to score? The second I stepped off the train, onto the St Pancras platform, I no longer felt that urgency, that disturbing, all-consuming need

.

Swollen pulsing clumps as the throat clenches, a gritty poison sludge globule comes up green black grey with every hack. The bottom row of teeth all cramm'd in till they're pushing each other out of the way (by gum) and all blood spills out of my mouth. Strength now my boy... rise up and claim this the very day is poised in still chaos, all before you...

1st November 2011

It cannot be infinite, the chronic, abusive consumption of drugs, of crack cocaine and heroin.

Medically, physically I mean, there. There is an inevitable and very consistent conclusion to this insane of inane bombardments of the senses and of the soul. And so it is time to wind down this messy habit, this horrible adventure. The Professor of Smack himself is advising an immediate cessation of the long-running programme.

This is how they felt after the last ever episode of Colombo was screened. Actually the repeated watching of the Colombo boxed set almost pathological has it become... The almost mechanical way that I now sit through the same shows again and again. It bears similarities to the way in which I pursue this life of sincere drug addiction. The ecstatic sensations that once came from piping and smoking are severely depleted as are the pleasures that came from the enjoyment of the original series of Colombo and yet there is no evident let up in the watching and the narcotics.

One more thing, R.I.P Peter Falk.

Awoken by the patient, ever delightful, Lil, sat disinterested as they come in the early morning traffic in Camden High Street... It is the 11th day of the 11th month of 2011, and aye we will never forget. 'Lest we forget'.

Last night I finally made it to see Astile, although I ended up chucking little rattle tattle pebbles at his window, trying to wake the little fella up, being as it was 1am...

Fucksakes – I really hope I haven't gone and done it this time (drama queen) my fucking left hand feeling like its being put through a rusty old school mangle. Indecent pain that throbs all about the wrist and the back of the hand. In difficultly adjusted positions the pain abates and yet fuckery fuckery fuckery is this I have unbearable pain in the wrist.

OK, an hour later and the agony abating positions no longer abate the agony... this particular hand has probably had enough of the abuse.

Back in the day (fanfare) an old faithful had set up home on the left of the upper hand... recently however it has been painful and painstaking to get a good solid wallop in the old five-fingered flapper.

Woke up today with a reduced version of last night's agony. The hand is still extremely bad... the area that I contrived to bang up in despite continual alarms from the body... sirens of high pitched warning signals that should've had me a bit more wary of going in that network of veins on the back of the wrist and hands.

Names and faces ransacking my thoughts

Texts exaggerating skulduggery in the frets

Made curious by the spurious

Need to achieve a victory to make myself victorious

Momentarily happy and glorious

OK, so the hand hurts but it wouldn't hurt to get back to those that keep your levels of self-esteem up by the attentions and attempts to meet up...

Dial with the other hand!

It's my lustful heart that leads me and my judgement that deceives

Bee-line

Bee-line

3 blind mice

Well I was a 'fraidy cat

Run and ran from my own shadow

Of you my dear I already knew

You were everything I wanted

And I knew not what to do

Nervously, I asked if we could do a tune.

My heart is damp but drying

My life's a mess but I'm trying

Rousing buzz of nervous ballooning noise reverberates around the ears and spirals, not nice, about the eyes.

Tufts of flesh flow out of these, slightly unsightly on the right jaw of the famous face.

Paris roars past my window, swamps my veins crushed into my walls, saunters away, goes to work in the morning outside.

La vie de Bohème:

Ah, I remember you – you were wearing fishnets

'C'est quoi, fishnets?'

I draw the picture.

She asks if I was wearing them?

'Yeah'

'Non!'

Stick it down

Fuck it off

Cough it up

Get it down

Bet your life

That which never was to be

Won't be now, will never be

Just as you always insisted

I always thought that somewhere, somewhere, somehow

Love – would – find-a-way

Aah, that gutless feeling overcomes me... en route to a Moscow venue. The first proper gig in quite a while. Not counting the drunken punch-up at Le Tigre or the sweat box that was the Macbeth show a couple of months back. So sorry a sensation. So sick my heart.

Truly I can push no more, or I'll be lying on the floor

breathless, death, yes

Nothing more…

Is this to be the final score?

Seeking strength now

The night at length now

Deeply entrenched allow

The understanding of this deplorable routine…

Now strike, luxurious and loud

Rousing the crowd

Making the rowdy suddenly rousingly proud

United, delighted

Under melody's glorious shroud

Back on the road or more precisely the U.K. – heading across the English Channel toward Blackbush and then Reading Festival, the fifth in this little run of solo gigs.

We have squeezed in a French festival between the Reading and Leeds shows. In Charleville, birthplace of Rimbaud.

Adrian, Iain, Kenny, Octavie, Céline and myself up above the white fluffy canopy in a quite raucous little propeller plane. Eight-seater, the only way to travel.

Squelchy sickly mucous cocaine in my mush. I'm sure the co-pilot saw me messing about with a $100 note in my nostril.

Have been trying to work a few new tunes into the set – is going rather awkward and slow the tunes are, just not thoroughly worked through.

Feel pressure.

Must try harder.

A spectrum forms on the aero's plastic windows and through the band of various filters a silver blue glitter that reflects off the wing. In a gap in the layer of clouds you can see the scale-like surface of the sea. The clouds' shadow is darkly outlined on the water.

1/9/12

Chateau La Fortine, Saint Emilion

Brassy, tarty, not altogether breakfasty

I mouth the shape of smoke-rings thick and cokey. Blood blots all over the fluffy white towelling of the bath robe. My chest heaves and hacks up slumps of snotty black lung soil. My nostrils leak dangly strands of liquid, speckled with tiny crumbs of chemical candy – remains of the many lines hoover'd up the ol' hooter this night pass'd. My left hand creaks in agony, craters carved into the skin with flesh-melting mounds of pain. A web of stringy lines of blood patterns the back of my hand. They sprout out from the wrist...

I remember the old man coming home from night duty in the guard house, lunchtime, 11'oclock. Heavy black boots and full soldiers get-up he fell himself on the green settee and closed his eyes and cocked a leg and let out a ripper and then in a slubber jabber slapper and looked at me and exclaimed 'Rats'!

'No that was you!' says I, and I run to him and dive on him and lay atop of him and the music to *Grandstand* fires out of the tele, you know the one?

There's a canvas propped up at the end of the bed. Naomi in a flimsy dress – natural girl look. She's beautiful. Clara's at the foot of the bed, perched with masses of blonde hair. She knows people in Essex who wear 3 pairs of false lashes at a time!

I must describe the technicolour vision of that sweet, sharp-toothed sort, how she is to pounce upon me and never let her claws go of me until she has temporarily exhausted her lusts. Describe the heavenly melodie that I play and sing as she pulls a grenade out of my cock with her teeth. The pair of us in ecstasies and narcotic bliss...

Céline and Octavie are in their pajamas, ready for an early night. Drew has hit the sack early too.

Yesterday's recording: 11 - aye, eleven - new demo's for EMI's attraction.

Stephen Street is on board me thinks for 2 weeks in March for the recording of the new Shambles album. For an autumn release perhaps.

For the first time there will be a number of Doherty/McConnell collaborations on the record.

I awoke just after midnight, in my own bed, in my rue de Copenhague chambres d'Albion. Wander in a daze into the kitchen.

Is it not impossibly wrong that I scratch and scrape at my own half-healed wounds and woefully wonky layers of blistered 'openings' – the only word that volunteers its honest services; a reliable account of its history, its work ethic to date is essential.

Closure must follow if the story concludes with a medical success and a middle-of-the-road values, moral-majority, vote. On this occasion I say hurrah for the very dead centre of my middle core, long may health and prosperity reign upon my fuck'd up forearms. By gum I appear to be a bent-back'd, scabby, snivelling leper this night, yelling curses and bullying at sweet ballerinas.

By Christ I need a hand out of this paradise and fast.

By thunder, my tea is getting cold.

Deplorable, I reason. Imposed to the last by similar numbness and casual entertainment with my trinket mounds, each room aloof to the other in self-sensationalised splendour and oh, wondrous oddities, complimentary beauty notwithstanding and tat.

Clinging on, albeit not in vain, all-be-it to move forward, shimmy on upaways and into understanding and into the light... I wonder, suddenly I am impressed by a standard issue curiosity. Where on earth am I going? Where is this taxi taking me? Thermes? In pronouncing the town's name aloud – 'Ter-mez' – the question mark seems to wobble and bulge and morph and become more polished. Neon flashes dance about the back of the dark taxi as we pass through a tunnel along the southbound périphérique and towards Ter-mez towards the Charlie Chaplin girl. Jesus, I'm damned and I'll be hung at dawn if I can't remember her name...

Rule Britannia and eyes down for a full house

'Ere – have a drop of brandy, son?

Poor fella

Now look

Never be the same again

Master of the self-inflicted wound

Carney

Whole panoply of them

The old brain cells lost in battle

Row starts from nothing

Bricking it before the Festival Hall

Thought it could have been the end of him

God knows I struggle with the shows

I struggled and it shows

And I'd hate for that to be

What's the entertaining thing about me?

He wags a finger –

'This one, she's a bitch'

He finger waggles.

'Waggles' being a wonderful word.

Estelle, always known as the Charlie Chaplin girl, left on the platform of Bibliothèque François Mitterrand.

And now I roll on through the tunnels, under Paris to Gare Saint Lazare. 'Tis unpleasant the feeling of something hanging over your head, a debt, a guilty admission yet to be made... I feel like a guilty man.

Naturally, momentum is given to the energies at work there by natural reserves of paranoia and introspective disquiet.

And so the train belts on through, this dusty, oily metropolitan Sunday morning.

Elspeth, heavy bejewelled pen etches the words, it's the baton. That way out of breath. Hope passes on through a last ditch lunge… an unlikely alliance, you pale, pretty, perfect, I do declare.

And I… and I and I am, I suppose, a wretched sight.

Indeed I asked you to be my girl, and you told me that you were terrified of me… what kind of an answer is that?

'I mean it in the nicest possible way,' you say, and smile and laugh.

Nelson Algren – The Man With The Golden Arm

Some find themselves through joy
Some through suffering and some through toil...
Johnny had H now, tried nothing else but whisky, a process that left him feeling like somebody new everyday.

Going past the RBS building just west of Aldgate East. The sound of sirens. We are crossing over from London EC to London E1. I'm meeting * ... owe him £600. A volley of abuse came by text when I woke up today. He'd come to Camden to collect at 4 this morning. I was asleep.

I'm on the balcony at Adelphi Terrace, just off the Strand. I think of Embankment Gardens, down there below me and the river Thames, a stone's throw beyond.

I do not feel sentimental. I just fondly recall times when Carlos and I would loiter about these side-streets. Acting out for each other in the mini amphitheatre round. Our ever present guitars rattling out new compositions. We believed them to be masterpieces.

It would turn out to be accurate – innocently arrogant and brimming over with belief in each other and in our unseen allies out there in the city.

On the SNCF train from Brussels to Paris, having played at a Belgian festival last night. I think that it went well enough. Dropped in a couple………that is to say that I 'dropped in a couple of new ones'.

Was great to see all the old gang, Iain, Boydy, Adrian and of course Katia who travelled with us and stayed in my hotel room.

Hmm, thinks I... could I... a bankroll of readies secure, in fair, if generous, recognition of my contribution to their esteemed publication.

An article that necessitates advance payment as the piece concerns 'flea markets', Porte de Clignancourt Paris & Billy Bilo's trinket-laden, antique-addled adventures in the divinity and infinite diversions of north Paris's most delightful market.

Ouai, ouai, viva les marchés!

Indeed this very ink I re-decorate the vicinity and me fingers with is a (post) deal breaking gesture. A glass pot of the cheapest Quink thrown in with the tins, nibs, stems & silver pipe/watch accessories that rattle about my brain and pockets.

Fuck you

Fuck you

Fuck you

Fuck you

Fuck you

The power is infinite but you have to know how to use it
Electricity, liberty, LSD

Don't leave me – it's alright, I won't leave you hot and... shut the door, lean the sideboard up against it...

We need all the evil old souls to die
The young must be strong
Fight for all they want
Liberty and pleasure.

Alarming how so lumpy
Are the arms

Masochistic, sick
Apocalyptic, fix n lick
Fix n' lick, lick lick

Endless lip suck sips
Molten oily pips

Sticky strips off in rips from bloated crust-coated limbs
So these were meant as hymns
      to the spirits that seep about
Moody and broody
Wits sharp as knives
All about may they be
      if influential in our lives
For God's sake my mind has turned itself on and
      mangled all the rails…

A boy named Sue is falling apart

Anne? Alize? Adam? F. H. Adrian? Andy?
Now for the names beginning with B......................

A funny one there last night.

2 saucy little things pounced on me between the stage and the bus. One in particular clung onto me like I was life itself, covering me in kisses and caresses and thinking that not only was she in love with me but that she was my love and that I was a genius.

Some may argue that such a wanton show of (possibly drunken) emotion is a less than attractive introduction. I say much the opposite. Youthful zest and overt sexual energy combined with a genuinely beautiful young body.

So anyway, they managed to get on the bus... slightly awkward a moment as I stood on the steps of the tour bus and said, 'Aye, these 2 are fine' to the security guards, poor fellas mob deep in fans and autograph hunters.

A quick snog later and a wee bump and grind to Hank Williams... and the ballerinas appeared. Say no more.

I think I got them on just to see if I still 'had it' or whatever, and the feel of nubile young hip bones wiggling all about the show, ah maman. I should have got their number. These hotel rooms are ok in the dark. And I want so bad to rag the ass off 2 young Italian lasses.

Been listening to the Beatle's anthology and it is curious how similar the sound is – of the early melodic rock and roll, live takes, *Kansas City, Can't Buy Me Love* - how similar to the sound we had in the early days of the Libertines. But then we were Beatles-potty in them there days...

We've got one of these [Eiffel Tower] in Blackpool!

Urban Clash Studio :

In session, Peter Doherty produced by Alain De Wassen

Stesh, Wednesday 27th/Thursday 28th March

Penny Arcadia Hard Times (No Sunshine)

Running wild amongst the artists and intellectuals in an existential tangent.

So I have to drag out this dirge

Because she will not say a single word

I'll carry on, vanish, vain and absurd,

Chasing, chasing birds

The old kicking up a stench of nooses

Rott'd with sweat, knotted with guts

With remorse and regret

And cold acceptances of every snapped neck

Every Tyburn 2 step

Did it cross the lines,

Were we out of time?

Something – the water I'd wager – lies stagnant in the pool.

And you, Miss, I wonder in private, are you here?
Does god see the girl you drowned?
Tucked away.
I can't imagine feeling like this all the time.
This behaviour, this way of moving.

I want to ask you so many questions, I don't know what I'm doing, I'm in love with you.

And bright ideas, folly-proof plans tail off, whirl away, spinning the strength of strategy thinking, the confident, cool stare now grinning, smirking in uncomfortable pride wounded, fanciful flights grounded until further notice.

For the foreseeable future of forever.

There's a hollow roar from a speeding past truck sounding for all the world like an unsympathetic crowd.

And so I'm here, shouldn't I gather myself and scarper? What is it that I'm after?

Endless kisses, for her to be my missus aye and its but silence, stunning brutal silence, acts upon the heart, the central nervous system like violence, on our alliance not a one.

I must be coming to resemble a stuck record I only observe and implode with frantic obsession the splintering and staunch silence.

What it is – I feel like I'm being greedy or selfish by being with you because I'm (uh-oh, wait for it) older, been around a bit and I can see things that you can't see.

I can see that you are a fantastically gifted girl, heavenly beautiful so beautiful. I want you & I know that I could (ugh) be with you but you don't know what to think, what to do.

It's a magnificent adventure, the start of a glorious life. It's like I'm pushing you to be in love with me.

Either you are incredibly strong or very carefree, I don't want to suddenly have you realise that it's all just a song, so... I know I'm hopeless.

Sid's Cackle

Sid's avarice, crookedness, and all around criminal scheming nature is highly exaggerated in the early Hancock radio shows. Creeping about the west London suburbs with a sack full of lead and assorted pipes, tiles, railings and even bits of guttering swapping some scraps at the breakfast table for a bit of grub. As Galton and Simpson honed their craft, reached the heights of highest comedy writing, so Sid's character becomes less caricatured.

Geneva Tuesday 31st Jan 2012

As luck would have it…

I ran into a lovely, be-freckled girl called *

Who knows how to score apparently,

Good job too cos I was on the verge of taking a

Subutex (shock horror!)

A good night all in all, did 3 new songs

'Birdcage'

'Nothing comes to Nothing'

'Down For The Outing'

London/Channel Tunnel/France 1st February 2012

Some manner of trepidation and exquisite joy filled my heart yesterday as Elspeth and I spent the best part of a strange busy night, staring at each other, in embrace, kissing, embrace, staring, kissing...

And the ladies came down the premium aisle with refreshments, bespectacled businessmen fill up the seats, faintly grey, very comfortable wagon.

David dropped Elspeth and I at the station and his own brand of refreshments I replenished my Paris stash with.

5th February 2012: It would seem that, finally, Sylvie has finished the editing of *Confessions* and so the first screening for the crew awaits...These last weeks have been the last chance to add some of my own music to proceedings. I have played *Perfume* (a sweet melodic little instrumental) as background pitter-plucking patter to the first love scene that my character 'performs' with Ms Gainsborough. All slow, sincere strokes, arched back and Charlotte's dignified character. I prance down the wooden stairs and out across the fields. Elsewhere at the end of the film I perform an acoustic version of the new song *Birdcage* that I co-wrote with the erstwhile Suze Martin... she has of late been seeing (romantically I mean) Mr Wolfe who has been diagnosed as having 'Saturday Night Palsy' and he's also getting evicted from the flat he was renting at * Camden High Street. But I digress...

    The film being finished now, and is, I suppose, about to be fed into the swamp... such a sense of trepidation I feel awaiting the critics appraisal of my efforts in this field essentially 'period costume drama' . Alfred de Musset for 21st Albion 'To pun or not to pun' is the question on all their inky lips I'd wager, regardless of those qualified, of merits, they will undoubtedly make up their mind to hate or love the lifting love story that is 'Confessions'...

Clatter of a million feet on crowded city streets gives a good back beat to the strains of sirens and smashes of the traffic as it passes, clogging up the cities roads, like a poison clogging up veins. Putting a time together (and in green if you don't mind).

Sally and I sit at the kitchen table in rue de Copenhague. It has been a while since I saw her last and these few days following the premier of 'Confessions' have been a wonderful chance for us to enjoy the company and companionship of true old heartfelt friendship.

Slight pangs of self-conscious guilt and shame when I pipe in her company and yet I feel at ease and very much myself when we are together.

She has been in all kinds of states and in the 16, 17, 18 years that we have known each other I can perhaps boast that at present I am in as good a position in life as I have ever been.

April 2012

6th Friday, Brixton

7th, London wedding, Alan & Eliza

9th Luxembourg

10th Belgium

11th Holland

17th Reading

18th Frome

Supercilious – one thinks oneself superior to others

Levity (noun) - treatment of a serious matter with humour or lack of respect

Extemporise – to improvise, work off the cuff in performance

Ectoplasm – substance left behind by medium during a séance.

It so happens that Elspeth is a little treasure in the kitchen. Makes a delightful change to be eating meals at home for the first time in I don't know how long. She bakes cakes too!

When your shadow blanks you
You know you've put your foot in it

Something ever so red about this here splatter – the heart of the matter this still chatterless après in-store skulduggery stint of what is the first day of the rest of my life…

Oh now, if you please, please just tell me what you see…
What's seen in staying so cold and sinister so and so.
Of course it matters to me.
Spit it out…
Spit it out...
Woh, wow! If you please, take me any place but Coventry – I speak purely figuratively
Can get pure mentality
Cut it out – leave it out
Do I need to? You really need me to?
Must I must I must I spell it out.

I'll sort out many things

Many splendour'd things

And when his lordship sings

He really sings

Really, really sings to me...

Lawless youth, unschooled, uncouth. No true belief in any truth. England's lost souls matter to me.

The professor is called urgently to Paris and seizes an opportunity to put Miss Plinth through her paces. It seemed too good a chance to let slip by and when I learned that the French capital was never before on any Plinthian itinerary my excitement doubled.

Get an eyeful of that Miss Plinth!
Embrasse in Paris! Saw you going to the Loo (vre) geddit!

Relive *The Rebel* in Montmartre.

Carries Deutche! Identity card.

Speaks! Polish! Also the tongue of the beloved Fatherland!

Unassuming life in NW1 Kentish Town posing as a secretary.

Lifestyle? Goes to gigs… infiltrates Bardic circles esp under der Linden Tree.

How many pipes for Miss Plinth? Sips tea on Eurostar like an English girl.

The King of Failed Rendez-Vous

Loves his title too much
To ever wear a watch
A captain Hook of sorts
He fears naught but
The ticking of clocks
Ticking of Glocks
To him as vague as snowflakes
Each second
Has its own duration
He's a time killer
Liberty lover
Won't let time kill her
The king of failed Rendez-Vous
Loves his title too dearly
He'll never concede to being really
But another late boy
Fate's toy
So don't hold your breath cos the
King of failed Rendezvous
Will never come meet you
For he loves the glory and the wealth
Too much to ever walk the line
And be a simple subject of time.

'You that pipe and you that play

You that through your hearts today

Feel the gladness of the May.'

                                        William Wordsworth

Holmes The Meddler

She dropped a thick black veil over her face and glided from the room. Ladies, y'know, they used to glide.

'See that you keep yourself out of my grip' says a bad-tempered man before bending Sherlock Holmes's fire poker into a folded piece of steel. Holmes scoffed at such a feat and straightened the poker up with his own remarkable strength. For Sherlock Holmes is regularly presented to us by his creator as a street fighter more than capable of looking after himself and skilled in martial arts and the fighting techniques of the East.

At dusk we saw Dr Grimsby Royshott drive past. Slamming demented fists. Deductions, coincidences of dates.

'Holmes – I seem to see dimly what you are hinting at.'

Sticky or, rather, oily flakes of cocaine, mixing at the back of my throat with the dusty grains of grey-green 'China White' heroin.

'Humanity though dignity. Systematic intimidation of individuals by institutions, regimes or governments.'

Justice Jackson, Nuremburg prosecutor.

Nose up in the khazi of carnage on the Paris-London Eurostar.

I must confess the menu is original on this service.

Sea bream with coconut milk and lime (!)
Beef stew with African spices & carrot flan (!)
Prawn brochette, Chinese rice, salad and Tom-Yam sauce (!)

This evening I refused to choose and indeed the friendly girl gave me a serving of each dish.
Little platters of everything. Lovely.
Washed down with a mini bottle or 5 of Médoc.

A burst of civilisation indeed, friendly, pleasant service after a week beset with violent incident and unpleasant exchanges with assorted Parisians including a lad of about 19 or 20 who grabbed at me, urging his pal to batter me, only for the other guy to be too fucked up on some heavy downer or other to be of any use in battle thank fuck... The sober guy was fresh faced and handsome. Evil cunt. Street robber. Mugger. Little would-be thug. Gangster.

'It is a swamp-adder!' Cried Holmes. 'The deadliest snake in India.'

Eyes resisting the light

I lurch on through the night

My stomach is sour

My thoughts are sweet

My jacket and breeches tight

So light a candle, let her long, young fingers grip my stem again and her old, old eyes from under wild hair dare me to be concerned about her age.

Aye, she taunts me as she pulls me close to her under these bloody sheets, these reet petites the freshest young French thing I'll ever sing about, I'll ever swing for and the hardest on and then yeah I spout and she clamps her soft mouth all around it and glad and happy as she drains the slow to droop lil juice coup to the dregs and then slides up my kecks and says 'Hmm my favourite'.

Ahuh! Skaggy spunk – the sweet young punk.

School in three hours too! Catholic is her institution 'Notre-Dame des Missions Saint Pierre'. Trop ... * is divine in form, dark of eyes – though grey blue they are, dark like paint. Red lips and nails, the breasts sweet and pale, far beyond words, a couple of words.

*L'opium est une saison**

Opium is a season

Le fumeur ne souffre plus des changements de temps

The smoker no longer suffers from the vicissitudes of weather

S'enrhume jamais

He never gets a cold

L'opium a ses rhumes

Opium has its own colds.

écorché vif

Skinned alive

Marriage has damaged * *, he fears the defective impulses of all women. Speaking of all women, * enters the room with Lulu on a rope, the feisty terrier…

'Monsieur Burr?'

'Are you writing a story? Hmmm?

Je pense fort à toi

You are not which one?

The rest of them are psychos saving lives… must be good souls brought together.

10th May I think I'm right in giving that date.

Just got onto what would have been the 4th train 'we' have missed. I say we cos it's Octavie and I who evaded the barrier of uniformed ticket inspectors on the platform and leapt aboard the SNCF train.

She is not to blame for our tardiness however. This is my area, my speciality. Hers of course is dance.

And so we head South to join Céline in Perpignan. Their home and my home in many, many ways. Warmth and family vibes all round. I have passed summers here, passed out here, passed strangely divine days & nights living around here.

'Is granny spry?'

'Round here she is my old mate,' and its clear why that should be so.

Meanwhile, Maison de Bonheur, and the rock n' roll grannies cannot be roused from their peaceful Catalan summer slumbers.

I am turning Mademoiselle Escure's mac's volume down a bar or 2.

Louis Armstrong sings *La Vie en Rose* and aye, as Aurora lays out her blanket at today's brocante, the birds whistle and lively little perishers to a tweet.

The cult of him he lost his bite

He got bitten and he lost his bite.

Wilhelm, born 1027/28

No sense of humour. Enjoyed hunting and the occasional juggling show. He was really excellent at hurting people and reserved his most murderous rages for anyone who made a joke about his horrible ugliness.

Anxiety & destruction

Gulfs in the gut

Belly wet with teary streams

I don't spend my time with anyone else.

But collusions with those old friends, they seem bound to each other.

So what do you say to that anyway?

I confess to the sin of 'adultery' though in wedlock we are not.

I think it's worse than me getting off with someone else.

You in that pen-knife triangle and them throwing you crackled crumbs and you're having a lick o the lickle ting & ting and me there, somewhere else entirely.

I confess to the sin of pride – I delight in being myself...

I can't lie to myself when it is plain and simple.

I can't be trusted, or shouldn't be trusted with the tenderest, tenderest loyalties and affections.

Out of sight, out of mind out of my mind.

Swindling swine.

First, second, third hits missed and then looked closely at my lump-laden forearm. All the while I had been thinking on the disappearance of all the old boozers from Whitechapel High Street and actually from the whole world. From the High St of the whole of Albion, such consideration distracted me considerably from the delicate job in hand... then wham! A fat old wiggly worm in a region that has always bemused and bamboozled me in many a set to... with me making to jag the junk and my left arm leaving me cursing the limb entirely.

Whallop! A flood of purple black frothy jetting ferment. Not entirely organic sounding but then this particular barrelful is now getting on for its past by banging date.

Once the junk and combined coke speedball is mixed with the blood of the first shot it's a race against the clock to get the remaining concoction in the blood-stream.

By the time the connection is made, the syringe is entirely maroon and one is invariably well into the great cussing period of intense frustration.

Thomas de Quincey famously refers to the 'great yawning period' in the early days of opium withdrawal. The expression appeals to me greatly, and I have elected his idea to cover all angles of detoxification and dinger related proceedings.

You'll end up in a pie or summut if you keep this up...

Cette conversation est stupide.

Elle about au désespoir.

This conversation is stupid.

It can only lead to despair.

The melancholic servitude of a world without light and life… all is stone, heat is gone, rehabilitation of hope through good English algebra… 'we're all doomed'.

Praying for salvation

Let the healing start

Miracles can happen

Take care of you

For you

For me

For all the people who loves you

The reason is a gift

You deserve it

Have the courage to believe

Think! Think! Think!

Learn! Learn! Learn!

Fight! Fight! Fight!

Believe! Believe! Believe!

Life is good

Thanks...

I give you my address

*69, rue de ********* Paris 75011*

Write to me

I love you

Sylvie

There has been some fantasy talk that is now shaping up for a crack at reality. It concerns taking the cure and kicking this suicide mission for a bit. Finally escape from this escape. This road has too few exits and the hard shoulder is hard.

Editor's note – *On June 27th, 2012, Peter travelled to The Cabin rehab clinic, in Chiang Mai, Thailand accompanied by Andy Boyd. Voted by 'rehabs.com' as one of the most luxurious rehabs in the world, The Cabin were keen for celebrity endorsement, a rather unusual attitude for an allegedly care-centred environment.*

The Cabin's aftercare provider, Cameron Brown, told the press, 'We don't allow time to rest and recover as such. Peter will be in treatment from day one and doing psychotherapy groups in the mornings, one-on-one counselling as well as holistic therapy like meditation, relaxation and massage, all the things that make it a whole treatment rather than just simply focusing on drug addiction.'

Mr Brown whose surname is also the street-slang word for heroin in the UK, added that Peter would be receiving Cognitive Behavioural Therapy and optimistically concluded, 'I think he's probably seen enough of the clinical environment of most centres and wants to experience life in full colour again.'

Resembling a sumptuous hotel and promising elephant trekking and yoga, The Cabin makes no references to the arduous process of withdrawals, despite boasting a 96% completion rate.

After just 3 weeks with nothing but a wooden Buddha for spiritual assurance, Peter was asked to leave for being disruptive. No mention was made of the bad dreams and shadows that crowded his thoughts, worried for his son's future, and saddened by the death of his film-maker friend, Robin Whitehead.

Peter arrived back in the UK late July to a flurry of negative headlines regarding his eviction from rehab.

The stint in Chiang Mai was not Peter's first time in a Thai rehab. In 2004, he entered the stark regime of a Thai monastery but this too failed, as have stays in Clouds, the Priory, and The Meadows in Arizona, not to mention other modes of treatment including implants, substitute prescribing and the Criminal justice system.

Brought back from Thailand a measure of faith anew in the possibility of being clean. Of getting clean and staying clean. Vow'd to do no more blood paintings too.

The sentinels are still, and the monkeys relax.

My guilty rehabilitated body struggles back into the game after 3 weeks in Chiang Mai, pitted with the rapid fire jaggling… and burning and infectious selfish abuse, craters and cuts and careless wreckage.

A terrible energy impacts, coiling and tightening, spoiling and frightening. But there are still now gentle splashes in the sunlight, midday in the dusty Pyrenees, across the frontiers through the mountains to St Genis Des Fontaines...

The sun belts down hard on the Catalan plains, I am sat in a big black rubber ring that seems to be gently sinking by the second. There's a hole in my Lilo! Damnations, blast it and fuckin' buggery.

I am in better spirits as my holiday enters its second week and recovered as I have from my 'Mal de Tete'... I had an epic bout of electrical pulses and warped abysmal pains in my skull.

But some days have passed, and I am much the better for it although my left hand is still swollen and horribly painful. My index finger resembles a big pink sausage emanating from my otherwise tanned body; a twisted pink sausage.

Met a lad in the chemists in St Gen's today. He had LSD tattooed on his arm and so I took the plunge. Like *'s father's friend he nips across the border to Spain for his gear. I took his number. Perhaps he's going across the border tonight. Perhaps I'll join him unless our wires are crossed. He can get white heroin in Spain and all the rest.

In the meantime I sit out in the bright, colossal and conquering sun on the decking of Céline's family house in St Genis des Fontaines... both her grandmothers are about. One, 'Nanna', is 95 years old and has a small room off the entrance hall. She has an extraordinary story of her life in Apulia and Rome (She is Italian); the other, 'Jacky', is a true charmer, knocking back the whisky and singing old songs.

During family meals everyone gathers round the big table in the garden and it's a proper sense of communal family vibes.

Fabio, Céline's sister's Italian boyfriend is staying at the moment so it's a true cross generational... the parents, grandmothers, daughters and two guys, two dogs, a parrot and the occasional 'tope' (mole) that Pieatra finds in the yard.

The garden is dry terrain with hose pipe irrigation, hammocks, the pool...

Love the taste of Grenadine. Sugar colour glistens in the silence, the dog and the child, the dust is wild. Some peace falls now on the heart, in the head.

First taste of family life, real family life, in some time. All my plans have been made in hotel rooms and bedrooms and on kitchen tables.

In fine spirits today despite unsuccessful attempts to purchase Le Coke these 24 hours past. The guy I met at the St Gen's chemist came up trumps with the old gear but did all the coke himself I think. I went to see * 's cousin in Argelès-sur-Mer as he was packing up his seaside smoothie and ice cream stand. Police and gangs of drunken beach bums roamed the 3 a.m. resort.

Am I really so entirely boonered that I have created the whole scenario in my bloody imagination? Whilst I was bashing away at the guitar I head a cacophony of calling and caterwauling from the street below up to the kitchen window. It sounded like laughter and a fracas from the girls (C&O) and the gaggle of fans who have apparently gathered outside our Parisian flat.

The thing is there was a very sudden -------------- boom sonic boom jolt – followed by silence – tranquility but it was an unnatural void. Eerie, too sudden, as if some shocking insult or gesture had suddenly turned the whole atmosphere sour. Strange indeed.

Thing is... the way things are at the moment, I wouldn't even ask them what was going on...

I feel I am coming to the end of my time with the girls, my beautiful ballerinas.

Silly, petty, boy-induced reasons...

I ain't got the strength to stand up to me

- cos I'm guilty -

Basking in the glow

Of a wanted man's gaze

I'm no spring chicken but I'm game

I don't wanna feel like...

...Really

Sometimes I feel like killing myself

I ain't gonna lie

Stick a knife into my heart

Because it's better to die

Than feel this way

Mother fucker gone & killed his

soul

dignity

Time and time again Céline shows a curious side of her indefatigable character. In her pajama shorts 4 night-shirt or whatever (usually a sunny look but in these precise moments she looks Hayden-Mcquirt) she makes a playful attempt to dig for some manner of fuckery...

Am I wrong to wonder that the presence of another girl in my arms is enough to send her a little askew...

So I'll leave her to it

He so wants to do it...

No more of that shit now, Pete...

'Moi, je suis fatiguée,'... Céline lies back and closes her eyes.

All is still in rue de Copenhague. Nary a mouse is stirring. Nary a frog is heard. The New Year fête has been and gone.

Mademoiselle Cippolat is returned from her family home in Perpignon.

I wish I knew exactly how I felt, although it'd be just my luck to have announced that 'deranged' emotional indecision … could that definitive statement be all that I long for and desire?

Don't worry – it's long since past caring there's no sense in stressing.

Had a most disturbing dream, I was on a game-show on TV, gambling with the oddest things, like love and life and everything.

You hear that crackling sound, a low thud and crash, and then sparkling and crackering and spackerling all around, like a pane of frozen glass suddenly headed off by the sun at the pass and the splitting of splinters, fever-fast like a flood or a rash, and finally the pane does smash.

3rd March, a beautiful Sunday afternoon, Céline is moving out of rue de Copenhague, staying at her mates' and generally sofa-surfing the social waves of Paris until she secures another gaff. We are now finally agreed it is for the best. Our friendship is a little strained, friends living on top of each other. 99% of the time is tranquility and harmony itself, two lovers who became friends and occasionally make love. But when its war... it's war. But despite the fact that we are not together, I cannot bear her to be with another guy in the flat, jealous, possessive, a few times now I have turned suitors from the door...

See the ratcatcher

A mind bent on rats has he

Blind with shattered glass is he

He leans drunken into me

Whispers filth and diseases

Death & agony

He empties his sack on me

And rolls on into infamy

Words of solace and sympathy for the stiffening corpses…
Feed and dribble on the memories of the past.

Your work is all but done
But there is still some England left in France

I ain't got the long capability
To say what is wrong with me.

New songs fuel the fire,
And the day of high wind
Starch the canvas to
Strengthen the flow

Finally made it to the train
tho not entirely sure where I am...
As unconventional as that sounds, nor do I know where I am going...

Home, perhaps… gaining an hour, light loss

Paris will be dark and wet

When I get there, I'll try and avoid breath monster who is at his same post...

Once I gave him a crisp £50 note and in doing so set the bar very high. Now, whenever I pass through Gare du Nord, he leaps upon me crying, 'My friend, my friend' –shouting for the whole of Paris to hear. He tell me that he will kill anyone who fucks with friend 'Mr Pete' !!!

I must be going home.

A Spanish-looking girl sits almost opposite me. She is scribbling in a note-book. She wears a quite distinctly patterned top, or is it a short dress, or a long jumper? It is white wool with silver and red roses embroidered across the knitting. She wears white tights and ankle desert boots with tassels and a red scarf. Stylish, very cool, outfit.

Vainglorious and wallop'd I be, the site all around the flat in Athlone Street, NW5, now framed with scaffolding and meshy nets the three-storey blocks of council flats and the soul free falls without fearing the height.

    The builders spank planks against piles of tiles and seldom tell each other much more than say a sly pun, a direction, or now and here and there again an Irish fella will burst into song. I make that four melodies so far this cold sunny day, January 2013, including a croony blast of Sinatra. I'm sure his big old boots did a wee shuffle and jig even his as his voice staggered ditties…

    Always seem to be a steady sweeping song of emergency sirens in this part of town, in this part of the play.

    I've more or less lost you. I mean you're not really here after that. Two full, flapping pages of earache from the very heart of the gloomy diaries.

    But really, how you adorn your pessimistic moods with a distorted styling of the body, the collapsing bed even.

    The half-hearted hope for the taste of these poisons to lose their addictive and lovely layers of flavour

Dutifully, I am in attendance to my… duties.

An album, a shop, a son …

H.A.P.P.Y ? Sketch and so

Am so close right now

Payments of debts?

*   *   (also n.bs postal)

*   *   (police custody)

Katia's birthday present

Bang bang bang bang

The measured heartbeat

Excitement and expectation

Is all that matters

The grateful and greedy

Faith ↗   ↓ hope   ↓ Love

Tour Diaries

Tour Diary 1

'You made me so happy for a second then as well… I thought you were coming back into bed with me'.

I crawl across the duvet. Pristine and white in the new morning. A sense of Arcadia surges like fast shadows up and gone. 'Bed' is sprayed in purple sprayer hair dye that has lain dormant at the bottom of the trunk since we picked it up from the Pound Shop, Brecknock Road some weeks ago… them bleedin' pound shops are lethal – you go in in all good faith to get a lighter or a stick or two of sandalwood incense and come out an hour later laden down with more heavy bags than that woman I've seen pushing a shopping trolley down Shaftesbury Avenue, humming (stinking) and humming the theme tune to Beverly Hills Cop. Bumming copper coins, smiling a cracking 2 tooth gape of a smile that lights up her tired old face somehow like a broken light bulb lights up a dark bunk. Until the moment you realise it is fucked, there is a sense of expectation. Could she be an undiscovered literary genius? An English Emily Dickinson, sans the comfortable life? With a rare and remarkable relationship as baggy-rights Maggie-trolley-tripe has with all the pile-up of pigeons down the pedestrianized part of Trafalgar Square.

Anyway, fuck all that... I was saying – I crawl across the duvet and offer my lips to my love. As she closes her already sleepy eyes and reaches for me with warm arms, her warm body... I spray cold water all over her head and run off, type noisily and abstain from the post-coital cuddling that I know she desires, that I myself desire... that will be heaven, that will be my heart's most tender ting on the heavenly 'to-do' list – that will disengage me from any activity ever again for as long as I live.

Jaysus himself wept... I always say this, 'Her love stops me living' and so what is living when it'z around? For life without love is a sad charade, played out amongst the oppressed and the oppressive.

Tour Diary 2 September 13th, 2013

Wake up arm in arm, heads on chests... the door... 'tis Adrian. We leave in 45 minutes for the next show, down the road from this hotel, in Oxford 02 academy.

When Katia got out of bed to answer the door I roll'd over to the right, only to realize I was resting the back of my head on a glass full of champagne cocktail... and not a drop spilled. Aha tis Friday 13th pack the trunk... listening to the album (*Sequel to the Prequel*)

Fall from Grace

Live gig in b&w

A band, Babyshambles comes on stage, with a very hostile crowd as public. They start to throw things at the band. One of the guys has a paper that says in three-inch headlines, 'Mick Withnall hurts people's faces' and shows it to his girlfriend. At that moment Drew tried to get off-stage but a roadie pushed him back; three-inch: 'Smack crack Babyshambles front man, bad boy steals hungry monkey his snack'. Another headline: 'Babyshambles new drummer is extremely bad-mannered towards sweet old lady and ex-prisoners of war'. Drew: 'Babyshambles bassplayer addicted to hillbilly dwarves swampoilsuck'. (Daily Star)

Tour Diary 3

Opiated aye... but even supine in my oh glorious otium - otium cum dignatate. Do not give dignity to the flaunting of ease... think nothing of it, let it be unseen, sunk sinking into ossification like the grey oil in the sharply bitter throat your water osseous old piper sat slightly in discomfort. Crackback. Only song is immortal – the words returned to the gods who celebrated their gift of sound and the worn but well intended words they welcomed home into their godly gobs in the glorious kingdom of heaven. No one spoke in heaven, sound was song and sublime symphonies soaring out of orchestral camps and pennywhistles but even pennywhistles sang sweetly, sad, serene, sweeping or celebratory celestial ska & skiffle & spurts of thick spittle streams splashing any poor sod unlucky enough to be tested by the gods and their manipulative scripting of all scenes in eternity. Testing angelic spirits to see if any of Satan's sick fucks were in town. Thousands of years of bedevillry and dictated – mostly demented daily delegated details for the oh devilishly loyal demons deranged but entirely devoted to Dr Bastard (aka Beelzebub) ... Where is this going? Oh yeah, the infiltrators made a right nuisance of themselves in the sainted exalted atrocities and glades and cornfields. Ah fuck this....

Tour Diary 4

Something disconcerting about Leeds shows traditionally... yeah I know it's in my head but it's in my fucking heart as well. This is the reason I was looking for escape routes (fantasy roams) right up until the last moment I fucked around with the busted zipper on my hold-all and moped down carpeted stairs onto the sun-warmed concrete of Copenhague (rue de)

    And to Gard du Nord

    Bladderful of pinkspecial

    Woe declared mohair whistle reck'd and torn.

    Speckly suit wet through

    From the swamp of Geordies

    Gosh the pit of moshers

    Long time down

    Reaching up grabbing at thin air mostly

    Facing fuckload of faces sweat-sticking hair

    To fallen fans that being an abbreviation of fanatic

    Old devil sea... waves and the feedback whips a crack

    So what's this now? Pesky torture.

    Cabin fever already? Sort yiz-zen out mucker

    There's a way to go as yet.

Tour Diary 5

I think we are in Leeds. The tour bus rumbles with a low whirrish static. Everyone's in bed, in their bunks except for Mik and meself.

Familiar scenes of detritus and debris in the ShambolioBus backroom. On the big screen Nicholas Cage is running through a swamp with himself (on screen twin). Take a nervous peek out of the window, blurred with bubbles of rain. Raindrops. Falling on Yorkshire. My body's a little contaminated, given the relentless battering it's been getting – chemical warfare in effect, some strange, slow, indirect suicide.

Might take up another hobby. Sex and ? and Rock and Roll. Fill in the missing word.

Tour Diary 6: Liverpool, 9th/10th September 2013

After a whopping old kipple at the Country Club on our day off, I was on a mission this night to adhere to the promise made to Drew and Adam to be done with the onstage violence and threats to harmonious flow... to try to fall into the music, be part of this band... sleep being conducive to the plan, it worked out all well and good methinks. Arrived in time to get on stage but 3 minutes later; the Merrylees were buzzing about backstage, eager young pups from Edinburgh. Well dressed young Dandy mods, one of whom was telling me that Bert Jansch had given me a shout-out at a gig afore he died a few years ago. They play a Coral-esque shanty-sounding set – the T-shirt they gave me is their band name plastered across an anchor. I'm not sure that they're going to be playing anymore support slots on this tour but I'll give their demo a listen.

Normally it's a pissed-up cluster fuck backstage at the Liverpool academy. Remember Uncle Arthur last time doing his Derek & Clive accent and shouting obscenities at the top of his voice. Was all cleared out tonight. Hot-hot-hot on stage, passionate crowd, by the time we burst into Fuckforever the whole place was jumping. Dispelled any concerns that my own reserved and measured manner was ruining the show for some people. Like they won't enjoy it unless I'm smashing up the gaff, the drum kit, the entire civilized world. The truth is that most people come because they are music lovers and want to hear music played well, in a tight and unified formation by the band they've paid to see. Probably seen more than once, probably more than once.

Set list from tonight:

Delivery

Nothing comes to Nothing

The Blinding

The Man Who Came to Stay

FallfromGrace

Doctor No

Loyalty Song

Farmers daughter

I Wish

Killamangi ro

Pipedown

Minefield

GangOfGin

Fuckforever

Seven Shades

New Pair

Penguins.

Tour Diary 7

Is a red letter a thing? I got to thinking it was. No reference points. 'Red letter day'... it's a thing isn't it?

Does it mean a day of great news?

Like a pools cheque or a day of ultimatums?

Pulsing blood, threading warmth, life through the body music. Sombre splendour of this crush.

A sense of eternity, the pattern of life – crumpled but recognisable. Inarticulate lads bound by their class. They don't get lost in Beethoven, Wagner...

Rock and roll. Our folk, our blues, our devotion.

Englishmen bent on the discovery of the sacred. A 17 year-old girl on the crush barrier, saw her briefly afterwards. She works in a jam factory. Left school at 14. Lives for music – says that Babyshambles, Libertines, me, lyrics, helped her through depression, boredom, through life. Her father died from a heroin overdose when she was born. Her mum hadn't let him see the newborn baby. He went home. Banged up. Checked out...

That bleeding back room on the tour bus.

Freezing it was last night. I was like a monkey in a fridge, in there. Roaring and moaning from time to time, unintelligible sounds of agony.

Tour Diary 8

'Tis a straight jacket – as oppressive as one. Nothing vague about horror.

Blurred visions of the future. Need to destroy; the thing bites into my bones, digs in.

Possibilities endlessly impossible

Sweat soaking my clothes, my face awash

Toothache in the heart – imagine the pain of that.

Tour Diary 9

Michael Whitnall is one hell of a man. A character no longer prevalent in the England of today, you might say the last in a long line of working class dandy heroes who used music, swagger and an over-sized cock to drag themselves out of the slums, estates and aye, caravan parks of this great nation's underbelly gutter swamp. Dark desolate places where intelligence and ambition are despised and the lack of meaning or control in the average life is a spring-board – usually to bitterness, obscurity and a vast reserve of unchecked negative energy.

The England we never seem to hear about in the colourful advertisement campaigns or even in the more socially realistic but ultimately optimistic portraits of great Albion anti-heroes. Robin Hood. George Best.

Tour Diary 10. 345678am September 2013. Manchester

Not sure what day it is really. Fuck knows exactly where I am...

Fuck knows a great deal of things

Knowledgeable geezer is old Fuck

Tour Diary 11. 8th September 2013

Day off after the Manchester Academy show last night. It's a little hazy but I'm pretty sure it was a fucking shambles in a Leeds-esque sense of the word. Pre-gig tension spilled over into tears – Stuart B was there and the pair of us were in a state, talking about what shit fathers we've been, getting angry and para...

Franny and 'Chelle were there too... Franny sporting a huge fucking gash scar across the top of his head from outside Wembley awhile back. Got a right panning I think.

Stuart's always been an intense fella and this characteristic has not abated one whit. I love him though. He sees right through me, right into my being. I like that.

Settled a bit now in this country club 'The Mere'. Eaten, bathed, sent clobber to the laundry... ah Drew and Adam the new drummer knocked... wanna know if the destruction on stage is gonna carry on...

Tour Diary 12

Welcome to the north... I was aware that Cheshire is an extremely wealthy place... this luxury hotel and spa with lifestyle magazines spread all over the gaff.

The bedroom doors open up onto the golf-course basically, or at least a patio just alongside a putting green. Can also pad along the path in my blood-stained slippers, along the way to some of the other chaps' rooms. Mik was pacing about when I knocked before. We all need a bit of kip.

2 a.m. now. Don't know whether to get into bed or get a taxi to Fallowfield and see if I can't sort summat out.

Scarface on tele.

Tour Diary 13

Ce soir nous (Babyshambles) jouons a Brixton Jamm. Jeunes filles, garçons, modpunks, scenesters, arcadian apostles, jostlers, moshers, wallopers, jollopers, bumfestivalis-savvy, the rejuvina and faithful (could it be thus) assuming the just this very moment released album – de-shambles has won over the hearts and minds and loyalties of the brating Girlish pub-lick adolescent aficionados of all things guitar warped wreckless clerics on their night off, sexless cherubs flown in from the oriental obsession – rich recruits to say nothing of the casual fans the ex-fanatics intrigued by their own reactions to a band that once had them under a deep and somewhat sinister obsessive state of hypnosis, random West London girls of great privilege and personal beauty (and height) who kinda dig the music but all in all just want to fuck a guy who fucked Kate Moss. Tick it off their list of things to do before the sun explodes.

Will I risk a secret text this moment passing sitting as I am directly opposite my true love?

Tour Diary 14: Lincoln 10th September

Black skies pushing in as the afternoon gives up. Wet and chilly over the cathedral and the canals. The sloping medieval English town-city. Full of butchers and swans and never the twain should meet for meat... the famous sausage sits proudly beside a blob of mustard and stuffing in my lunch time fantasy.

I seek out natwest – 'NatYes' as they call themselves in their new posters (9/10 mortgage requests agreed to) and a slim lass in flat red leather shoes. A fraud flag has had my account frozen. 'Did you try and pay for 350 euros worth of cocktails on the 28th of August?"

Think hard... nary the foggiest. Barcelona hotel rooftops and shit loads of pink Mojito's... could this be that of which they speak?

Next stop the Angel tearooms, wherein Drew and new drummer Adam are on their respective lap-tops around a coffee table. Pot of tea I fancy, splash of cream, two lumps of hard brown sugar. Under the table, umbrellas. Outside for a quick cough and a drag on a Gauloise. Down to my last packet.

My love must join me soon for I miss her so and life is too short... to go without her when I know she is the one I so worship and adore... after traipsings around, after and through and from love these three decades past, Pan,

Aphrodite and Dionysius have finally come up with the goods in the form of Katia deVidas, of life.

If ever I was to claim a wife.

Tour Diary 15

Angel Café – pot of tea under an umbrella in the rain...

Fat fella, northern, angry, bulging eyes, shouting or at least talking loud at/to his silent girlfriend. I take her to be a bullied, mousy wee missy and she rope-pullies enough pity from the well of my sentimental heart until I hear her pipe up : 'Ah shut yer fat fookin' cake 'ole Frank, yer al 'as spouting a lot of shit at me face.'

Everyone on the patio under the rain, under the umbrellas, looks up from their tea and coffee and cheese baps.

Frankie goes red, looks meekly at her.

'And don't look at me with them diseased puppy dog eyes either. Get...' She sucks on a Rothman's Kingsize. 'Stoopid get.'

'I love you.' He shouts back.

Tour Diary 16

Back on the bus, back o' the bus, I fuel and refuel the faithful annihilator

    This moment, these hours, these days

    The mouthful of mash-primed gumachine

    Seems somehow (if ever it was otherwise)

    Full of sham, flecking the rib of hambones with gollp-shame

    So crestfallen by the chemical continual

    Aye as ever continual sides of little glass necks coloured up the morning

    And up the motorway stoater of a pied-poker

    Ought to have floated all these glumdoomy detailings

    Far and wide of the page this type-written account

    But then I suppose that's the fuckery of the luck of the draw

    So duck out/stop to score

Tour Diary 17: 12th September 2013

Another break in the *Sequel to the Prequel* tour… and another plush hotel/spa resort to relax in. Given the level of emotional distress these past few nights, it's extremely timelyn'all

Bejabbers I'm at sixes and sevens… even Katia's arrival (heart-warming and spirit lifting) concerns me. Thinking of her with ten mostly sex-crazed geezers on a tour bus. It is all my warped perception no doubt. Her presence will subdue my restless spirit and assist the majority of the lads in their attempts to create a positive atmosphere on this tour. Dark and twisted dementia not being in vogue this early autumn (dementedness?)

BouBou bringing her natural and bountiful blessings of peace and aller son petit bonhomme de chemin. So then onwards, and indeed, upwards. Curses upon myself for even imagining the worst.

I always open up to Katia… offer her my mostly unlikely, but always heartfelt, theories about the on-going saga of on-stage upset. She says I might be bi-polar.

I argue that I only suffer such extreme devastation on stage, not in everyday life like genuine manic sufferers.

'Really?' She says. 'Once you told me you couldn't leave the apartment to post a letter.'

The debate continues.

Tour Diary 18

When I heard they were evicting me

From my own fantasy

An executive explained to me

How it follows demographically

And then the executive said

That I should try and be dead

By next July

Of course we'll miss you

But we can exploit and

Reissue

And sell footage of you snuffing it

To Sky

Faith hope love

Interview

Transcript of an unpublished interview with Peter Doherty by Nina Antonia. Hackney, London, June 2012

June 24th 2012 at Red's House, Hackney, East London.

Peter Doherty (P): Live from Percy Mountbatten's dormitory!!

Nina Antonia (N): *When did books, literature, music, become important to you?*

P: When I realised it was the only way out of the situation I'd found myself in. I grew up in army barracks most of the time; it was stifling, intimidating, army uniforms and barbed wire. I did have a laugh at school, though. The first poetry I liked was the war poets: Wilfred Owen, *Dulce Et Decorum Est,* 'the old lie'; George Orwell, *1984, Keep The Aspidistras Flying* and *Down and Out in Paris and London*, particularly - I liked the idea of this man in the 1940's coming out from behind his desk and going out into the world, I found that appealing. When I turned 16, I was like a greyhound out of a trap, I wanted to get out of school and live with my Nan in London. My dad wasn't having any of it, but what could he do? I'd come of age. I couldn't stay in that environment. Talking to kids now they just don't feel confident taking off to a new city, getting a job behind a bar. Now it's so much more difficult to get a cash-in-hand job, find a flat, find a squat, the world is so much more sterile.

P: I seem to have spent a lot of my creative time contradicting myself, searching for liberty whilst imprisoning myself. The process of creativity rejuvenates the spirit, it justifies existence; having a couple of songs on the go, that's fulfilment to me, that's when the soul is healed. Yet creativity comes from melancholia... when you are happy, when you are living life to the fullest, then there is no time to create. You don't need to, because you are living life.

N: *Prison? Is there anything about that you could describe as meaningful to your creativity?*

P: Only in terms of clean time, I wasn't out scoring drugs, it's a hard jones, prison is carnage, brutal all boxed up. It's an endless cycle of violence, humour, sadness. It's an unbelievable cross section of the underworld and also the screws as well, putting loads of unstable people in little boxes and then sitting back and watching them. It's carnage. We had a prison band, I played guitar, there was a dealer on keyboards. All the blokes in the yard would press their faces against the windows to watch us; they'd be going 'Doherty, he's shit'. I always thought it would give me the time to think but the only time its quiet is at night, at four in the morning, then I'd make a cup of tea, sit back. Then it's peaceful. But it didn't change me, no.

N – Was it difficult, the adjustment to fame?

P: I was living it already in my head so I was prepared for it... but it was a fantasy. All that happened was reality became a fantasy that I'd had. That we'd imagined, dreamed of late at night, talked about, conspired over, through the songs that happened. It's a strange business becoming a public figure. By signing a record contract, by putting yourself in someone else's hands, you immediately cease the way of life that created those beautiful songs. There's only so much time you've got with that original spirit before, by necessity, you change. I could see it happening, I could feel it happening, that's why I got out, that's what happened with The Libertines... they were quite happy to live in a way I couldn't, so they edged me out and tried to carry it on for as long as they could.

N: So you created a new environment that was truer for you?

P: Basically yeah, truer for me but it excluded a lot of people in my life because I went all out to the extreme... (sighs) I've often expressed my views of the Libertines as being on a conveyor belt – it's conducive to the industry not the artist; it's jobs for the boys, the same accountants, the same roadies, the same travel agents. Mostly they are bland people perpetuating their own system. I railed against it as much as I could.

N: That must be an alarming feeling...

P: Yeah but you are sedated aren't you? You're happy to go along with it because your records are selling and you're playing to crowds... and we never had. They saw it as a worthy sacrifice and so did I at first, but in the end I wanted the old feeling back and to be in band with people I could spend time with when we weren't on stage - as opposed to people who would only get together when we were on stage. I wanted to back to be with my mates, simple as that.

N: Did you win a poetry competition and go to Russia?

P: That story's got mixed up. I did win a competition for a crap poem about smoking... but the trip to Russia was for something different. I used to run a poetry night at the

Foundry on Old Street. Worm Lady used to read her work... there was a piano... we'd recite poetry and drink absinthe, as part of the Amphetamine Cabaret. We did an exchange that the British arts council paid for because we were skint. There was a club in Russia, The Dom, that was supposed to be doing a similar thing so they came over for a week... but they were more like a circus with dancers and fire eaters... then we went to Russia, we got a bit lost. I remember walking round Moscow in a long brown woolen coat eating chicken.

N: *Libertines?*

P: I can tell you the truth about that. We didn't really have a name although we'd thought about calling ourselves The Albion. Scarborough Steve was the singer and me and Carl had the songs. One night we were in Camden Lock sitting by the canal and we played this game. We finished a bottle of wine and threw it in the lock. Whoever hit the bottle with a stone could choose the name of the band. I can't put my hand on my heart and say that I hit the bottle but I will say that if we didn't call it The Libertines, we wouldn't play together again. The name comes from this really perverted book 'Lust of the Libertine' by the Marquis de Sade. It's an eighteenth-century obscenity. I had a cheap copy of it for novelty value,

During the French Revolution when the Bastille was stormed, de Sade, with his great big grey beard, wandered out with this manuscript of filth under his arm. I liked the L in Libertine, it was elegant. It was the right name at the time. I've still got the flyer from the first show we did as The Libertines. It's got a picture of Stephen Spender on it, sitting by the fire.

N (as an aside): Spender's last book of poetry, Dolphins was issued in 1944, the year of his death. Dolphins, Peter informs us, like humans, are the only mammals to make love for pleasure. He goes on to describe the mating ritual of cats, the male's penis growing thorns during the act of mating. Red, our host for the interview, donated one of his cats to Peter while he was living at Sturmey Lodge. Six litters later, Peter's country house was over-run despite the thorny process. When the sleepless watchman loses touch with nature then he severs himself from poetry. Peter has yet to read Robert Graves's The White Goddess *but has a copy.*

N: I saw you at Riverside, before there was a full line-up

P: What? You were there for the old school Libertines?

N: *I think there was a cellist; it was a night of poetry.*

P: That must been after Scarborough Steve left... although he showed up that night, out of his mind. He got chucked out of the band because he was always scrapping, but he came to the Riverside. Sometimes he'd turn up at shows, forgetting that he'd been chucked out. He was into the Stooges and the New York Dolls and said that we were like The Beatles, so when we got described in the press as being 'The Strokes/New Wave' he was like 'Oh fook!'

N: *Mystical Albion; is it in the blood, DNA, memory...?*

P: We don't have mountains but we have forests. I used to live in the past, was entrenched in it, the time when England had forests of oak; but when we conquered the world, and became an empire, the forests disappeared, and the timber was used for boats, ships. We are Elizabethans, that's what we are, surrounded by history. I'm not a royalist but I can't deny that I'm an Elizabethan. I'd love to go back to the Elizabethan age, to the time of alchemy and true adventure

When you got on a ship and set sail from Portsmouth and didn't know where you were going, maps weren't completed yet. Charts were being written by Englishmen and Europeans.

N: You are a big aficionado of W.B. Yeats – You mentioned his poetry as referencing something akin to Blake's Albion, a quasi-mystical England?

P: I can't not be interested in anything to do with a W.B. Yeat's poem... I know it's been said before, but it is so richly evocative. It gets me every time. 'Slouching towards Bethlehem'... crawling towards Albion. Each one of us is on our own spiritual journey.

N- Distractions from the path?

P: Drugs can be a distraction, the business is a distraction... relationships can be a distraction: when I was with Kate, she was up there (gestures heavenwards) and I was down here. She wanted to control everything: who I saw, my friends, where I went. Everything takes you away from that pure magical time at the beginning when you are untouched, uncorrupted, when you are in your purest form.

N: Is there a price to pay for being an artist?

P: There's always a price to pay

N: Are there any more film roles that you're interested in?

P: I've just finished the film about Alfred De Musset (*Child of The Century*) and I've been offered a script to play a character that is the complete opposite: it's sex, drugs and guns. They want me to learn French and get a six pack... filming doesn't start until Sept 2013, so I've got until then, basically!

N: Did you empathize with De Musset in any way?

P: The script was so beautiful I couldn't not do the film. De Musset could be a bit of a dick sometimes... he got himself into a duel which he loses, which I didn't like, so I tried to get them to change it to him winning, but Sylvie the director, what she liked most about my acting was in the moments, the scenes, where I felt most uncomfortable and unhappy...

That's been the story of my life. She wouldn't let me go to acting classes! I like being directed, harassed... but not too much. Don't forget my dad was in the army, I grew up in army barracks. Sylvie came to see me at my old house, when I was living in the country. We did a lot of wandering about in the dark.

N: *Did you find Pan?*

P: No... street-lights, and one time a police dog. I don't know if I found Pan but he was always there.

Red: *Who is Pan?*

P: Pan is a Pixie God... of revelry, music and nature. He originates from Greece. He's a spiritual survivor from the age before technology. All pop-stars in the modern tradition that capture the imagination of young people especially are Pan-like. Bolan was a Pan-like figure. Young people still have that complete love and passion for music. They queue all day long to get down to the front of the stage, to be in touching distance of their demi-God. The music is like Pan's flute and they go skipping along, chasing the melody into oblivion.

N: How do you feel about going into rehab?

P: Really confident, more so than ever. It's the right time for me.

More titles from **Thin Man Press**:

THE RISE AND FALL OF THE CLASH
By Danny Garcia.

In 1983, punk band The Clash split at the height of their fame and success as relationships between the musicians imploded. The band's original members, associates and friends, recall those crazy times in frank detail as forensic film-maker Danny Garcia unravels what really happened.

'The whole story, warts 'n' all, told by those who knew them, those who were there...' Kris Needs, Rock journalist and author

SPARK IN THE DARK
By John Constable

The first collection of verse and dramatic prose-poems from *Southwark Mysteries* playwright John Constable. The volume showcases Constable's darkly controversial, high-octane, epic prose-poem, *Wenefer* - a retelling of the Isis and Osiris myth, set in south London's club scene (warning: sex scenes, bad taste and oaths) - as well as political satire and lyrical romances. Constable's 'urban shaman' alter-ego, John Crow, adds strange histories from London's Cross Bones Graveyard where the 'Winchester Geese' (sixteenth century prostitutes licensed by the Bishop of Winchester) are buried.

'Like Shakespeare on Acid' Time Out

A WAVE OF DREAMS by Louis Aragon (book/cd).

Louis Aragon's 1924 surrealist prose-poem-essay, is published here for the first time as a single volume in English. Aragon vividly describes the inner adventures, the hallucinations and encounters with the 'Marvelous' which took the young surrealists to the brink of insanity as a revolutionary new era in Art History was born. The accompanying CD offers spoken word extracts set in musical soundscapes by Tymon Dogg & Alex Thomas.

'A leftfield treat...mysteriously opaque and strangely lovely.'
Thomas H Green, Daily Telegraph.

LICENTIA by A.A. Walker

Licentia is a fragmented journal, an 'artefact of desire', a kaleidoscope of erotic portraits, intersecting relationships, encounters and hallucinations. Baroque characters in a variety of psychological guises people a romantic dream that makes the heart race.

'Licentia has a compelling staccato lyricism recalling Dylan's Tarantula in its hallucinogenically layered and fast moving narrative. An hypnotic Beat Fable whose protagonist seems collaged in fragments into a whirlwind present day scenario created from disorientating romantic desires and unreliable memories of distant times.' — Alan Rankle, Artist.

All Thin Man Press titles are available on Amazon, from bookshops and in e-book format, including Kindle.
www.thinmanpress.com